Dᴿᵒᵖᵖⁱⁿᵍ Bombs to ~~Feed~~ THE ₕᵤₙᵧᵣᵧ

[An]thology

Edited By: Lauren McDougald
and
Corrin Donahue

ISBN: 978-0-6151-8817-1

Acknowledgements

This book began as a series of handwritten poems on loose-leaf paper compiled in a folder. Before long, it became clear that the talent of these students needed to be showcased on a much larger scale, so here it is. These students have demonstrated in their poetry that they have experienced far more than most of their peers or teachers would ever realize. In spite of their struggles, they remain wonderfully bright!

I would like to thank all of the students who have shared their innermost thoughts, fears, dreams and daily musings on the pages that follow. I would also like to thank Crystal Baker, Matthew James and Tykera Granby for typing the poems. Last but not least, I would like to thank Lauren McDougald who personally took on the challenge of compiling the poetry, editing, illustrating, and creating the final layout of this book.

-Corrin Donahue

Bam
     Bam
          Bam

Twenty seconds into creation
And our frames were
Systematically paralyzed
Mun.key[s] sat themselves
Up side Down and proceeded
To munch on Ban.and.A's
While golden fish floated
Casually in their bulbs
Wondering: "How come evolution
Forsake us to this little bowl
Full of our own crap? Oh look a
White castle. Must we filter
Feeeeed for the rest of eternity? Oh
Look a white castle."
Cue the trumpets; this victory
March must be our grand finale
Since we are all about finalizing
With finesse and letting our
Maledictions and imprecations
Blow off into the other us surrounding
Like dust on our hands

You know, they
[the men in the green suits]
Say we are soooo full of grace that
We oughta carry ourselves like the
Disgraced tomb of
Omega Wah Ha Hu
Who? Yeah no one knows her
Anymore cause she was stiffly fingering
The air when all the hoopla
Of "create me create me" was going on
Like the petulant priest she was
And we are for being in her likeness
Not giving a damn about
"yes, no [or] who done it"
But really
Just shoot me
give us that rush
[us as in all of us my cells and
their cells and the cells we create]

Of the big bang when
My existence was that
Of coexistence
And normal was simple
Metaphysical collision after collision
Suspended above an ending that
Sees no end because the
Provisions of life are well contained
In the circular loop of humanity.

-LE

This anthology includes the creations of the following artists:

Brandon Alexander

Yo! This is Brandon, the guy behind the words of compassion and sensitivity. I'm 17 and I'm from Southeast Philadelphia. Most people call me Philly because that's what I talk about and represent. But, I try to represent the good side of Philly and not the side most people talk about, like gun violence and death. Also the main thing I love in life more than Philly, is girls. So that's what I choose to write about in my poems. My mother and father raised me to be a gentleman and that's what I am. If you read my poems, that's really me talking. I'm not pointing fingers and saying names, but those poems come straight from the heart.

He Can't See It

You're being hurt, but he can't see it
For all that you're worth, and he can't see it
You're a star baby, but he can't see it
You're a grown lady and he can't see it
You would stay faithful and he can't see it
You are so playful, but he can't see it
Girl you're the bomb, and he can't see it
Even cared for his mom but he can't see it
You act different ways but he can't see it
You're crying for days and he can't see it
Baby I'm here and you don't need him to see it
I'll treat you so much better I just need you to see it
I know I'm not the first but its ok I see it
I'm everything you want; all I need is...to be it.

This Position

It seems she broke my heart, by not even calling
I can feel myself trippin' but not even fallin'
Like a punch to the face, my heart's in a daze
Seems we broke up and went two different ways
My tears are cold but they burn like fire,
From my eyes they roll away like an empty tire
Down to the ground, they form a puddle
I feel I am being punished as if I'm in trouble
Maybe I messed up and did you wrong
But I'm dying inside and it's been too long
I can't take it, I know. It's over, you win.
I don't wanna be in this position ever again.

City of Brotherly Love

I love Philadelphia
I love "The City of Brotherly Love"
But my city has a darker name,
"The City of Brotherly Slugs"
Because it's so dangerous I don't dare
Visit for long periods of time
Making that place a permanent residence
I would have to be outta my mind

I love the food
And the diversity of all the beautiful women
But Philadelphia, aka "Murder Capital"
Ain't where I'm gonna be living
It's the birthplace of my favorite rappers:
Cassidy, Joey Jihad, and Reed Dollaz
But it's also the main place you
Can hear mothers' screams and hollers
See them holding onto their son
His body lit up with bullets
Stretched on the pavement
His clothes and her hands soaked with blood
We may need to make funeral arrangements
But No!
In his mind he's not giving up
He makes it to the hospital still breathin'
The doctors are filled with amazement
Soon after the shootin'
Word is spreading 'round the hood
In each and every way
'Bout how the boys from 5th Street
Were gunnin' for Jaheem
They left his body after the shootin'
Because they thought he was dead, but he wasn't
So now all the boys in my family are out for blood

Jaheem was our cousin

"Yo Unc, I wanna ride out with y'all, let's go get these niggaz"
"No, you only 9, a youngbull, you too young to be pullin' triggaz
You're the man of the house, look after your two sisters and lil
brother" As they left I was standing there thinking "When are we
gonna stop doing this to each other?"

That's the dark side of Philly

Which pushes me away.
That's why Philly is too crazy for me to stay.

But the good parts of Philly
Is what I touched on a lil in the beginning
And I'll say it again
I love the food and all the gorgeous women
Blacks, Whites, Asians, Puerto Ricans, and Cambodians too
Not finding the right lady is a hard thing to do
It's the place where the sun's rise
Over the skyline is why I love to wake
It's the home of the muscle factory
Where I lifted my first weight.

Philly

Chris Ballard

I am Chris B. known as Chris B. #30 but referred to as Mr.Unfugwitable. I'm almost 17. I write poetry about my feelings at the present time. If it ain't what you want to hear or read....too bad, read it anyway!! I hoop in my spare time and I'm known as a somewhat flirt. Enjoy my poems and if you do, get at me, I don't spit but I can write off the top of the dome. Check me out....

I Was Only Dreaming

I was sitting in the car one day
Not making a sound,
No one was near me,
No one was around.
I looked outside
And it was completely dark
I started to get scared
I was sitting in the park.
All of a sudden
The car went BOOM!
And at that time
I knew it was my doom.
In an instant,
I saw my life
So full of good times,
Struggle, and strife.
I saw all that I did
To and for all the people I cared.
Never tried to harm anyone
Never even dared..
As I floated off to heaven,
I could only think, "Who...
Who would want to kill me?
What did I do?"
I looked down
And saw a face I recognized,
It was you!
You were the one who caused my demise!
I asked "Why did you do it?
What were you thinking?"
You replied, "Chris I'm you,
And you're only dreaming."

Life is a Dream

Man why is life so rough
Full of heartache and pain!
I want out!
Help me get away from this miserable place called life!
"CHRIS! WAKE UP!!"
I woke up sweating hard.
"Huh? Jesus?? How did I get here?"
Jesus replied, "You been here, brethren."
"What do you mean? I have been living life. DID I JUST DIE?!"
Jesus answered, "Life? Die? No brethren, thou were just asleep."
I replied shaking, "FOR 68 YEARS?!?!"
"68 years? Thou were in slumber for a couple of hours."
"So why did you wake me?" I asked.
"Father told me to wake you up, you were making too much noise."
"So all I went through in that 'life' was a dream?"
Jesus said with a smile, "Yes. Just a dream."
I said, "But all that I went through.."
"Just a dream."
"But My family.."
"They are in the other room. You dreamt about them?"
I replied, "I guess so…..good night Jesus."
"Goodnight Chris."
I spoke quickly, "JESUS! One more thing."
Jesus replied with a smile so bright, "yes brethren?"
"I love you."
"I love you too. Goodnight Chris."

My Talk With My Brother Eric

Chris: Kappa!
Eric: Sigma!
Chris: haha! What's going on my nig?!
Eric: Chillin chillin. You good my sir?
Chris: You know it! Hey man when you wanna go to the gym wit me, we ain't hooped in sometime now.
Eric: Soon man, work is a killer nowadays.
Chris: Yeah, I know. Workin with Stanley ain't no walk in the park neither hahaha!
Eric: hahaha!!
Chris: Eric, did I ever tell you how much I love you my dude?
Eric: Nah man, how much do you love me?
Chris: Well you know how they got them shirts that say, "Jesus said, 'I love you this much' and stretched out his arms far and wide and died for me?"
Eric: yeah.
Chris: Well I can't love you that much, cause that's a lot of love Jesus put out. But I love you almost as much as that. You my heart my dude, don't forget that.
Eric: Chris…gimme a hug my nig.
Chris: I love you Eric.
Eric: I love you too Chris.
Chris: Look, I gotta run for now. Try not to forget about me now, I'm only a call away.
Eric: I'll call you sometime. Take care and be easy lil brother.
Chris: ha. Lil brother. I like that. Take care big brother.

My Bae.

This girl,
Taylor Christina Dunn,
Is in my heart
She's a lucky one.
I've only seen pics
Of her beauty
And might I add
She's a real cutie.
We tried the going out thing
Once or twice,
Didn't quite work
Due to distance that wasn't so nice.
She is always there for me
No matter what the situation
She sticks by my side
No matter the complication.
She keeps me smiling
When I need a friend
Something tells me this girl
Is here until the end.
She can come to me
About almost anything.
I'll try to make her smile
or at least get her laughing.
She owns a place in my heart
And that's all to say
Meet Taylor Christina Dunn
A.K.A My Bae

Letter to Tadja

So many ups and downs.
Fusses and fights every other day.
Going to school not talking to each other.
Heartbreaks when going our separate ways.
You put up with my crap. I put up with yours.
BUT STILL!
We became the best of friends.
I get a big smile across my face when I see or hear about you.
I still remember the day you hugged me tight at Southern
Boundaries.
That was the highlight of my day.
I was so happy to see you that day. You just didn't know.
You are my nigga Tadja.
No matter what you do, no matter how much I TRY to be mad at
you.
You will always be my nigga.
I love you Tadja E. You are a gr8 friend.
Always there when I need you.
When I need a joke, a laugh, or just someone to cheer me up.
You are always there.
You are my nigga Tadja. Don't change on me.
Make sure we keep in touch. You are too true to forget.
Thanks Tadja E!

School Life

Bell rings,
Time for class,
It's early in the morning,
Still dragging your azzz.
Get to your seat,
Look at the teacher you hate,
But still you need this class,
To graduate.
You pay attention
Only for a little while,
Then A.D.D. kicks in,
When that girl gives you a smile.
Finally the bell rings
To go to your next destination,
You move slowly through the halls
With STRONG hesitation.
You stand with your friends
You feel like you wanna skip
But you break from them and go to class
So you won't hafta hear your mother's lip.
Lunch is nasty,
Taste like crack,
But you still eat it,
You don't take it back.
You've done your time,
Time to go,
But you'll do it all over again,
Tomorrow.
I Hate Being Late
Being late is one thing I hate
With a huge passion!
Why can't we be on time
In an orderly fashion?!
I hate being rushed
Unless it's by me!
Because when you rush
Isn't it a type of worry?!
With me, don't waste time
Being slow!
Cause when you're ready
Aren't you ready to go?!
I don't like people
Showing procrastination!
Don't they know it takes time

To get to the destination?!
Get off work at least two hours
And let's not hesitate!
It's just ridiculous
Why do I hate being late?!

Not a Bragger

I can play sports, but I'm not a bragger
I can learn a lot, but I'm not a bragger
I am smart, but I'm not a bragger
I can make a girl love me, but I'm not a bragger
I can learn fast, but I'm not a bragger
I'm a good worker, but I'm not a bragger
I can have fun with anyone, but I'm not a bragger
I can think on my feet, but I'm not a bragger
I like the way I look, but I'm not a bragger
I can be funny, but I'm not a bragger
I am a fun loving guy, but I'm not a bragger

I'm not perfect either.

Rick's Talk With God

Rick: Lord. I need your guidance
God: On what my child?
Rick: Well, life is hard with my parents.
God: Well in Ephesians 6:1 it says 'children, obey your parents in me, for this is right'
Rick: I try to lord, but they make it so hard!!
God: Well I watch you my child, and it seems to me that you bring it upon yourself at times...
Rick: what do you mean lord?
God: such as the time you back talked them when they were telling you right, it seems to be your own fault for disobeying and I found no favor in that.
Rick: But lord...
God: But nothing! It is written, therefore thy will be done. Remember, Ephesian 6:2 says honor them, which is the first commandment with promise.
Rick: .....You're right lord. What can you tell me about my wife? You know we have problems seeing eye to eye sometimes.
God: You love Ephesians huh? Ephesians 5:25 says 'husbands, love your wives just as Christ loved the church and gave himself up for her.'
Rick: I try to love her...
God: Try harder.
Rick: Yes lord.
God: Anything else you want to tell me that I already know?
Rick: No sir, thank you lord.
God: Anytime, I'm always here.

Teach Me

Teach me how to swim
Before I dive right in
And drown slowly while you aren't around
To ever see me again.
Teach me how to work
Until I can go off on my own
And show someone else how to work
Rather than leave them alone.
Teach me to be patient
With people who are nerve-wracking
Cause lord I need it
I have surely been slacking.
Teach me how to love
The word I play around with a lot
Telling these girls I love them
But all I want is their twat.
Teach me how to sing
Cause I do go and try
I want to sing to the heavens,
The heavens in the sky.
Teach me how to live
Because I'm on my way out
Teach me what this world and this life
Is all about.
Teach me.

Love: A Word We Play With

I tell you I love you
You tell me you love me,
But do you even know
About my true personality?
I see in your lusting eyes
All you want is sex,
Get your lil bust in
Then think "who's next?"
Why sit there and toy
With someone's feelings?
Don't you know saying you love people
Can cause so many suicide killings?
Why say you love me
And we only just met?
How can you be in so much love
And haven't got to known me well yet?
The word LOVE isn't just
For a nice saying or gift,
The word love
Is a word we play with.

Money the Root of All Evil

Our biggest enemy in this world is money.
Money is the root of ALL evil.
Instead of enjoying this God-given life,
We are worried about money.
BURN MONEY! It brings nothing but headache and pain.
Why do we always need money for things?
We can't enjoy a single minute of life....
Without money.
"Money can't buy happiness..." people say.
But the only time I see people smile,
Is when they have some money in their pockets.
Keep money....
Spend money....
Take money....
Steal money....
Kill for money....
Why?
....
Because money is the root of all evil.

Tina

This girl right here
Is my lil white lady,
Or in terms she may understand,
My lil white baby.
She always wants to talk
No matter what time of the day,
"She calls a lot for you Chris"
My parents would say.
She tells me she loves me
I tell it to her back,
But only the friend love
The relationship love, I don't know about that.
She's my white girl
I found my cure to jungle fever
I don't think I'm going to let her go
Nope, ill try to never leave her.

My Ears Are Closed

You think I am paying attention
To whatever you are saying
But really, I'm looking at you
And my mind is swaying.
It can be something so important
That I really need to be listening to
But I'm definitely ignoring what's being said
Just to spit out the truth.
Tell me about God
And I'll listen
But talk too long
And a lot of the stuff you say will be missin'.
Ask me what was just said
About three minutes ago
I was looking at you the whole time
And I'll still say I don't know.
I could just be bored quickly
Or I could have ADD
But talking to me,
Is like talking to a dead tree.
I'm nodding my head
To show you that I haven't dozed
But there is no use in talking to me most times
Because my ears are closed.

Calm

Right now I am calm.
I got a feeling I'm going to have a good day.
Everything is going swell so far.
I got my music with me playing.
I'm relaxing….
Not a soul is around to bother me.
People are quiet or not loud.
I got my soda with me.
Laid back in my chair.
The weather feels real good.
Food is in the kitchen cooking for me to eat in a minute.
It's peaceful……
I'm not thinking about working.
I could just go to sleep.
Not a worry in the world right now.
No anger for me in sight.
No frustration for me.
I'm just fine.
Only one word can define my state of mind right now.
And that word is……
Calm.

My Walk Home

Coming out of the mall
It was real dark outside
Some time around 10:30
I had no ride.
My cell phone broke in an accident
I didn't see a payphone
I looked in the parking lot and no one was there
I was all alone.
Since I stayed walking distance
My options were real tight
Either stay here until morning
Or walk in the dark with no light.
I chose to walk on
Not knowing what to expect
I was so paranoid out there
I WAS A NERVOUS WRECK!
I heard voices of people on the street
Some hookers tried to talk to me
They would say "sucky sucky five dollar?
I'll get on one knee."
People arguing outside of homes
Drug dealers selling merchandise
While I'm thinking to myself, "If I could just get home
That would be extra nice."
Seeing what goes on out there at night
Showed me I'm blessed
Having to live somewhere I don't like
Is better than living on the street and being stressed.
When I arrived home
I could feel total relief
What goes on out there
Made me lose my "I can make it on the streets" belief.
I'm A Grounded Star
Sitting outside in the dark one night
There was a little sparkle on the ground
It made this real loud noise
Somewhat like a breathing sound.
The sparkle made movements
It had eyes, mouth, and a nose
Finally this star made up its mind
And finally it arose.
The star went to do good things
Tried to make it in the life struggle
Had to do things that

Would cause him to trip and even stumble.
One day the star looked up
And saw all his friends doing nothing in the air
Then the star started to wonder
Shouldn't he be up there?
Did he really want to be up there?
Or do his thing from afar?
He chose to be on his own and alone
And said, "Because, I'm a grounded star."

Notice

He sits in class smiling at everyone
He is always the go to guy for advice and answers
He drives people wild with his positive personality
He never wants to fight, only befriend
He's the quiet guy in the room
He minds his own business when around people he doesn't know well
He sits back as if everything is right with him....
But it's not
Ever notice the little tear in his eye when he smiles?
Ever see how he puts on a fake smile so you won't worry about him?
Ever wonder why he's always there for you?
Why would he care so much for you?
Is he stupid?
No.
He was in love.
And I bet you one thing....
You never noticed it.

Fight

You want to fight me?
Aha what's good my dude?
You really don't know
What I have in stored for you
Do you have any idea what this means
To a nigga like me?
I get to take anger out on you
That I had for people in my own family.
What you just did and said
Was not the smartest thing
And here you go wantin' to fight someone
Who likes to laugh and sing?
I don't need peoples
But peoples you might need
Cause after I'm through with ya
Ya face will be on permanent bleed.
Enough of this small talk
Let's get to business
And believe when I say even if I don't win
I'll never be finished...
FIGHT!

Quiet Rage

Get away from me
Can't you see I'm sitting here quietly?
"What's wrong with you? Why you so quiet??"
I'm not smiling, I'm not singing, and I'm not in a riot
I'm in rage…..
Like an untamed beast been captured in a cage….
I'll hurt you
And you had nothing to do with it too
Someone had gotten under my skin
So I sit here with my fist under my chin
Biting my lip so I won't say nothing I'll regret
Shutting up so I don't mean any disrespect
But I just can't seem to escape
As violence inside starts to rape
My peaceful heart
I'm alone hoping that'll give you a clue from the start
It may have been
I was born with this out of this world sin
Of being the quiet staring blinker
And at the same time being the quiet murdering thinker
…Back up and leave me be
While I sit here quietly
Because I'm like an untamed beast that's been captured in a cage….
But to battle it, I stay in QUIET RAGE

Depression

I have something on my mind
So I decided to write it down
Let me let you in
On the reason I frown.
I hurt inside deeply
Manhood stares me in the eye
But I'm not ready to be grown up
The mere thought makes me cry.
Love plays too many games
And hits me in a hard spot
Makes me wanna throw away my heart
Let it sit in a corner and rot.
I can't focus on anything
Nothing makes sense anymore
Dying isn't on my mind
But my heart and brain lies by the door.
So many things coming fast
Like NASCAR
Happiness was all you seen out of me
But now happiness is so far.
You see me smiling
You hear me laughing
You think he's alright
But you don't know what's happening.
I'm not doing this for recognition
Not for a poetry contest
I'm doing this because I'm unhappy
No, I'm doing this because I'm depressed.

Expectations

Everyone expects so much from me
But that's just it
I'm only me
I only know how to be who I am
Expect me to do well
Expect me to be smart
Expect me to act nice
I'm only me
That's all I know how to be
Why do you expect so much from a kid?
People expect so much
From a guy who can give so little
I don't expect anything from nobody
So don't expect much from me
I can only give what I can
And what I can't give….
Don't expect it…
The Quiet Noise
Sitting in the room
Quiet…
Not saying a word
But saying so much
In it's head
Always wondering
Wondering about little things
Always thinking
Thinking about big plans
Seems quiet face to face
But making a lot of noise to itself
Says nothing for the moment
But soon
It'll say so much
And its noise inside will be quiet
And the quiet will be a noise

Michael Beach

Age 17
Junior
Hi. Well, this is supposed to be a biography type thing where I spill my guts and tell you about how great poetry is and how it's an art form and I'm blessed to have this gift, etc. etc.... So sorry to disappoint. Poetry is a way of expression, and it is far from aesthetic- being just pretty words. No matter how putrescently florid people may make poetry, they can never completely drown out the message and meaning they want to impart. I personally try to make mine either humorous or serious. I am very interested in politics, religion- even if it's controversial, I may just have an opinion on it. When it comes to poetry I like the stuff that makes you Think- many of my classmates have written such things. Excerpts from their daily lives, things that pertain to them- those are what I want to hear. Reality is the best poetry- and if someone disputes that with a "Roses are Red" bit, I will be unable to control myself from mocking them incessantly.

I often write about politics, or current items of interest. One such poem I wrote about is the rapid decay of the subjects of music. Not just hip-hop, but rock country, and all the rest. I do not want to make people sad. Nor do I wish to make them happy. I want to make them think. As humans it is our duty to focus our minds and intellects, and decipher that which we cannot understand. By no means do I hereby endorse any cruel experiments that people may have used this rationale to justify. All I am saying is this: We must further our knowledge that we have, by the means that we have. Why sit back and allow a small percentage to control the world? Knowledge is power, but comprehension is sheer might. To understand how things are, to see how they work- that is the most amazing ability of all. I hope you enjoy the poems that I have written here. And remember- don't just read- think about it.

Repression

When a light fades
Who is to blame?
The one who tried to unleash it?
Or the one who stifled it?
Regardless of the answer
The light is gone.
Happiness is never found
In repression of emotional identity
Even if the repression
Is to save the light from pain
The only people who are never hurt
Are the lights that have already faded.
Repression may seem a saving grace
But stunting growth is unimaginable pain.
And the meaning of growth
Is to bloom into whatever we are
Not to be cultivated into what others wished to be.
We walk this road that winds through
Darkness and light
In hopes that we may laugh at the road's end
No matter how near or far it may be.

The Crow

"There comes a time when silence is betrayal."
-Dr. Martin Luther King Jr.

I stood in the center
Of a Garden
Of statues made of marble
I sat and watched the human pass,
Wrapping his lips around deceit and hate.
He would recite to me
Such loathsome words, yet so moving
That I could not caw
Could not speak.
I wondered when he left, if I could have said something.
The echoes of his voice still rang
Harsh human syllables bouncing off of marble.
He came again and again, I listened but
Did not speak.
He made his solutions, and they made me feel vile.
I was privy to all of this yet didn't speak.
Because I could not confront this man millions died.
I was no raven.
I was stool-pigeon.
Then came a day when he returned.
He was cornered, frightened, asking my help.
I considered silence.
But I had been quiet for too long.
I said a word.
It was a human word I had learned so well in these past years.
'Die.'
The man became monster [or was he always a monster?]
Took aim and fired.
I flew from my perch, and landed before him.
No more hate, no more death.
But it wasn't enough.
That mouth had ended a race with its incessant speech.
I tore out his tongue, and brethren followed suit.
No more would he speak.
A man, different, came.
He tried to follow the former's footsteps.
I had learned. I proudly recited all the first man said.
The new one fled.
I had learned, and would no longer quietly betray.
For "there comes a times when silence is betrayal."

The Withered Children

I.
We are the withered children
So thirsty...
Our voices are dry and cracked
SO thirsty...
Our whispers of discontent under the demon's din
SO THIRSTY...
We are crumbling, shambling, following the wind
Water...
Left to decay, innocence stripped by a desert wind
WATER...
Watching the wind pass, feeling its sting, helpless
Wa...ter...
We cannot move we cannot talk we cannot breathe
W...a...ter...
Dust in the wind, we are accosted... we are lost
w...wa...wat...water...

II.
Now is the time.
Let the dirge be heard, a green sound
Our power a symphony of night
Our bass fills the air
Our strings play the tine
Dance tour music, o children.
Forget the old dances
Forget the rights you once had
Your only rights are to dance
or
die
Die in this ballroom
Dancing to the music of destiny
Ours
All ours for the taking
You will dance, for music is sweet
To us
Regardless of what you withered puppets dream

III.
A river
A red river
What happened?
Where are we?
What are we?

Did we do wrong?
Up has become down
Left has become right
In has become out
Light has become dark
Cold.
So cold
So hot
So tired
So be it
We are done
We confess
We confess your sins
Not our sins
What are our sins
What have we done?
Who are you?
Who are we?
This red river
That quenches no thirst
Rushes by, swollen with out
un
shed
tears.

IV.
A bleak tired sun Rise over the Pacific
Over the Indian
Over this waste
Over me
What is home?
Where is home?
A warm embrace
A gentle heart
So near yet so far
A shattered mirror
Presents my faith
For the world to see
I hold this iron
This fang
It has tasted blood
It desires more
I do not
I feel the wind
Wipe away my
dry

empty
tears

V.
We are the withered children
Stripped of our clothes
Borne by the wind
Dust blown by a flute
Of madness and power
Beaten off of a drum
Of hate and greed
Crossing red rivers
Of loss and pain
Watching the nameless crumble
Of agony and fear
Shattered faith
Endless red
This river must run dry
This nightmare must end
The music must fall silent
And we must rest our weary feet.

A Drop in the Ocean

Just- a drop in the ocean?
Barely noticeable, not even there?
Is that what you call it?
What happened, even if it was across the ocean?
Six million Jews, gone up in smoke
Five million others, ash in the wind
ELEVEN MILLION souls consumed by fire.
Is that a drop in the ocean?
The drop of blood between a newly stitched pair
Of Siamese twins
The drop of birthing fluid from a mother, legs tied together,
Screaming in agony
The drip of tears down a skull-face,
Life dying in its eyes.
Is that a drop in the ocean?
You would stand there, with your slurs and flags
And swastika-sucking, head-shaving, need for supremacy,
And call what happened
Just- a drop in the ocean?
Look around, oh ye of little faith.
You stand alone with your flag, alone with your symbols, alone
with your denial. We saw it. We lived it. We ARE it.
YOU are the drop in the ocean, and we are its waves.
So get real, get with the tide, or get washed away.

Why?

Why don't we care about the poor
The abused, the molested, the outcast?
The diseased, the starving, the lonely?
Why don't we care about the unfortunate?
Because
We are wrapped up in our own lives
Our hurts, our pains, no matter how small
Are magnified above theirs.
We may laugh at the less fortunate,
But it would be a lot less funny
If we looked at them and realized
"There, but for the Grace of God, go I".

Words in the Dark

Form darkest regions near and far
From heart-torn wounds and invisible scars
Eyes watch the moon in the sky
No time to live, only to die
A baby's wail, a young child's tears
Shuddering hearts quiver in fear.
But! An intricate design in our being
Unleashes a completely new form of seeing
In darkness a light does shine
A message to all with an open mind
No matter how deep the darkness there is a way
For the sun to rise and bring forth the day
For life and love to this end we strive
A voice screams out "Hope is ALIVE!"

Pledge

I pledge of allegiance
To the flag
Of the united oligarchy of America
And to the tyranny
For which it stands
One nation
Above God
Easily divisible
With liberty and justice
For rich, white,
Straight, protestant, men.

The Requiem of La Vie Bohemia

This is a Requiem, a funeral song
Of a death that has been ignored for far too long
Today there are no more songs worth hearing
Nest to none I find endearing
No one sings of nature or political issues
Let me find my tissues
For this sob song about a break up
For this ditty about a make up
For this song about a night on the town
For this song about how that makes him frown
Songs about cheaters
Drugs, sex and wife beaters
If it ain't smut, it won't sell
All these hoes are screw and tell
No more songs just about life
It's all about doin' the wife
No more are with reason
Reason is out of season
The season is heat
And it's all about forms that're sweet
Doin' it all
Music's takin a fall
Look in the mirror what do you see
Is it that music on TV
What are we teaching our kids today
Exactly how girl's hips should sway?
How the boys should "superman dat ho"
I just gotta say this crap's gotta go
No songs about compassion, friendship or life
It's all about drugs sex and strife
It's all about the money
Getting some from that honey
Spittin' about anything that sells
I'm just sayin' "what the hell?"
I guess by Benjamin Coffin the III it was best dais
"This is Calcutta. Bohemia is dead."

Carolyn Bell

It's So Strange......

You think you are close to certain people…..
You think you have a bond with this certain person
You find out in the weirdest ways
Who really cares for you and about you
I guess I must ask myself who is really there for me and who really cares for me
Does that person (the one you thought you had a one on one Friendship with, told each other just about everything) really Think it's going to be the same???
Think about it….we try and help people through ups and downs
We try and help people through the worst times ever
You sometimes hold back what you want just to help them out
You take them/ show them one of the most prized things that YOU have in your life
You gave them hope even though no one else does
I guess the past makes you grow
The present makes you wiser
The future shall never be a total surprise…….

How Do You See the World?

How vain is it to tell a lie just to make someone feel special
How dare the world try and teach children right from wrong,
when all they see is wrong........that soon seems right
How dare you stand for a cause then when it happens to you,
You go against what you stood for
How dare you try to blank out what's going on just to make your
World perfect
When you've felt you can't take it, and you burst out screaming
Rather than fighting how dare someone laugh at your pain
How do you sleep knowing that someone, something is being
Hurt every moment
How dare you look down at someone just because of their
Appearance
How unique is it to ask, "How can we take racism out"
How difficult is it to hear, "It's not my problem"
How dare anyone honestly say they are a true friend
How dare people give up just because they feel there will never
Be change
How absurd it to think everything will be ok

Lee Besant

Mister

Hey Mr. Crooked Thug Life Tattoo, Mr. I Roll With a Crew Over Honor Roll, Mr. I Hate He Who Consumes Jelly Rolls Though I Know Without Him Anyone Who Pleased Could Roll Right Over Me, Mr. I Write Poetry About Eating All But The Edible and Discredit the Incredible For Posters to Show My Face, Mr. I Don't Know My Name Nor Yours So Calling Us All Niggas Will Do, Mr. You Can't Be My Wife But You Can Be My Baby Momma and Boo, Mr. I Don't Know Two Times Two But I Know More Sentences Than a Judge and Won't Hesitate to Two Time You, Mr. It's My Mother's Duty To Raise My Baby, Mr. I Never Thought To Take Caution After Scabies, Mr. I Can't Go To College But The Army Will Help Me Be All I Can Be Starting With a Mathematical Degree, 1 Grenade + My Legs = No More Walking For Me, Mr. I Don't Appreciate My Ancestry, Mr. Long Straight Hair Is Pretty, Mr. All Light Skinned Girls Are Pretty and Dark Skinned Are Pretty Ugly, Mr. Hey Hey Hey Look At All The Thug In Me, Mr. Because I Smoke Weed I'm a G, Mr. I Party Like A Rock Star But Don't Know Who The Bands On My Shirt Are, Mr. My Car Sits Higher Than My I.Q., Mr. Because My Mother Is Too Sick To Raise Us I Have To Drop Out Of School, Mr. I Could Shut Down The Apollo But My Craft Won't Help Me Get The Lights On, Mr. All It Took Was One Night To End My Life Though I'm Still Alive, Mr. I Have To Turn A Blind Eye To What My Father Puts In His Vein At Night, Mr. My Son Just Hasn't Been Walking Just Right

I Write This For You

The Subway, The Space, The Music

She is in her own world and we'll never know of its wonders for
only the melodies and symphonic orgasms of her headphones
are invited, a simple tap of "play" button her eyes are ignited,
sirens, gunshots, winos chiming along with invisible choirs of
lives long past, all are deflected by that which morphs she into
the very reflection of music in motion, I see her head bop and
her eyes close as the sparks under the subway roll on, on the
other side of the universe, on towards even more distant planets
and stratospheres and she doesn't notice as she's steady lip-
quoting what seems to be the equivalent of an ancient
civilization's chant, bobbing and weaving through reality and the
actual sight of actuality, the scene is breath-taking as she
almost floats above the world, a city girl, I read her music's
graffiti on her face, a light hazy look, of the "take me away"
type, I can almost feel the lyrics, or lack thereof, emanate
soulfully from under her hood, and she is an intergalactic being,
not hood nor preppy, just alive and breathing, jazz, blues, hip-
hop, rock, country, music nonetheless, I kinda wish she would
bless me wit one of those earbuds (cuz you know my batteries
were those cheap Dollar General junks) so I could plug into her
temporary world and blossom from an 808 bud, maybe rub up
against her between verses, I'd use the headphone cord to wrap
around us and lasso the sun so that it may pull us from the earth
and into intricate drum patterns of meteor showers, the
synthesizing of stars that shatter, the skat of passing comets,
the low rush of the Milky Way, wishful thinking BUT, that is her
place and the space in between her headphones and ears and
aisle, and her blind stare that will never reach mine is too minute
for us to find each other, and besides, I've almost reached my
stop, and as much as I'd like to get off at her stop and see the
rhythm of her mp3 player projected in her walk I can't and I
couldn't hold her hand because she snaps her fingers and is
chameleon-like as she goes from smooth lounge R&B singer to a
gothic punk rock bringer, but wishful thoughts, I like her shoes,
she wears the graffiti Converse I wanted and a Bob Marley
purse, but there's no need to pursue because I gotta few CD's to
cop anew, but, maybe I'll catch her on the way home, feed off
her zone again or maybe I'll have new batteries then, who
knows? Damn I hope she's on the ride home so we can skate
Saturn's 8-track, I know she has some wayyyyyyyyy back music,
probably has harp for voice and Rhythmatic Flow for a name,
perhaps after all she could match my poetic rhyme scheme, her
lips on her song's mission move like a dream, shoot I wish I
could hear what I was missing behind that Jamaican hoody

DING "And we are now stopping..." I miss the rest of what the conductor is saying and all just to stay in her world a little longer BUT, I must cop my own slices of heaven, unlike her, I'll be willing to share them, Goodbye to She, the loudest silent songstress...

Jerel Bond

A True Friend

A true friend is someone standing by
My side,
All the way;
Always there to help me
Through the day;
Building me up when I'm weak;
Erasing tears when I cry;
Pulling me through
When I am shy.
You're always there through
Thick and thin.
A friend loves at all times—
I will always call you my
Friend.

The Final Kiss

It's my last day of school;
My life is a bus
And your friendship is the fuel.
But will this secret love
Last forever
Between me and you?
The final bell has rung
On the last day of school.
I waited by the door as
I asked my parents
For more time.
I looked to see we were alone,
And we kissed.
We kissed
Because we would not
See each other
Again.

Kendall Breeden

I hope you enjoy reading my poems. My name is Kendall Breeden and I have always enjoyed poetry. It wasn't until I was around twelve years old that I really started to write poems. I enjoy poets such as, Benjamin Hughes, Langston Hughes, Maya Angelou and a lot of others. I started to write my poetry about my life and what goes on around me. Over my life I have had a lot of good times as well as bad; however I still manage to make it through. I am doing all I can to not just be another African American citizen. I want to dare to be different. I refuse to let my name Kendall Breeden be looked at as everyone else's. I am my own individual. I have my own goals. I am striving to be the best of the best and I express that in my poetry. I sing a lot as well. I am in the process of trying to turn my poems into songs. It's a little more difficult than I thought. That's enough about me. Once again thanks to my family who inspired me to write. I would really like to thank my dad who has been there by my side (it took a while to realize that) but now when I look at it I see that when ever I look back, whatever I am going through, he is always there to lend me his helping hand; Also to my mom, who is not living, Regina Yvette Williams, I love you and you have been my other huge inspiration.

Life

Life is like a game, you must work hard to
get to the next level;
Life is like Grand Theft Auto, you must
survive to succeed in the world;
it is not meant to be wasted, you don't
have forever to live;
in life you take journeys in which you are
asked to give;
Life is full of choices
And please be serious don't play,
Even though life is like a game
One day you indeed will pay.

Where Is a Friend When You Really Need One?

A friend is supposed to be there always by your side,
Until I start to realize that when I need them they seem to hide;

I know that sometimes people may hurt you,
But please, yes please use patience it's a virtue;

so when you are wondering where is a friend when you really need one,
Look deep inside your heart and you will be sure to find one.

The Pain is Never Leaving

Those hurting days are back in my life, when
certain people seem to cause me strife;
It hurts when it comes, so I do a lot of grieving,
Until I asked my friend one day
and she said the pain is never leaving;
The pain is never leaving as I thought
And I cried,
Be careful who you may attach to
for they might not stick by your side;
I have to remember to let it go and stop
grieving,
For now I know that the pain is
never leaving.

One Day

I can't believe she is gone away, it seems
so strange that I just saw her the other
day;
I sit and I think and I wonder why, before
you know it I can't help but to cry;
I cant stop the pain it sticks forever, I
guess all I can do is hope for the better;
I wish she was here, here to this day, I
guess the best thing to do is continue to
pray;
One day we will see each other again, happy
with no pain as we rest in Heaven

Phillip Burton

I'm one of the best
But I'm under rated
When I spit, I'm killing
Like raid sprayed it
Cockroach haters
I know y'all hate it
To hear a man like me
Yea I'm one of the greatest
I speak what I spit
Spit what I speak
I go hard on the mic
Make the strong look weak
The top of the game
Is what I seek
That's why I'm climbing the charts
Until I reach the peak
And I'm coming up fast
I am the future
Y'all are the past
Y'all like a class
Y'all I just past
On the hip hop highway
I move fast
There's no competition
No contest
There's no one better
I am the best
I am right now
Don't care whose next
I'm a rapper with no flaws
Bulletproof like a vest.

The Best of All Time

Best of all time
Meaning from beginning to end
Don't take L's to the head
I'm in it to win
I am for real
I don't pretend
I don't know what that means
All I know is to win
They said Hip Hop is dead
So I picked up a pen
Me vs. America
Hand on the bible, I'm going to win
I love music to death
Pray that ain't no sin
Mix me with a beat
Hip-Hop the blend
It's simple
It's mind over matter
Cause y'all don't matter
When it comes to makin' hits
I'm the best batter
It's B.O.A.T.
Nobody can do it better
I'm getting cheese
Like cheddar
Money makin' machine
Three M's, one letter
I do it big, I'm a pimp
Put it all together
It's big pimp Phil
I'm fly without feathers

Girls

I'm all about the dollar
But I always keep a dime
If I ain't got a dime
Two nickels do me fine
I be hittin' on 'em
Like a punchline
I tell 'em
'Show me yours, I'll show you mine'
Like I used to back in the day
I was a lil mac
Macking each and everyday
In recess
I didn't ever play
Two girls took me to the back
And told me 'Let's Play'
I don't spit game to girls
I don't have to
'Cause they already on me
Like a tattoo
I'm bad with names
So I call my girls boo
They call me Phil
But Baby, out of school

Lefty

I'm not a good lefty
But I'm the best writer
I can spit in water
And it still be fire
I'm nasty on the mic
Like apple cider
And since y'all can't touch me
Call me a ghost writer
I'm flowing like a river
And my flow is wet
Like my Jay
Nothing but hits, Nothing but net
You can't tell me nothing
Like Kanye West
And since ain't nobody better
That makes me the best
I'm beating these M.C.'s
Punch before line
I'm killing my beefs
Time after time
Even though I don't try
Half of that time
I'm killing M.C.'s
Rhyme for rhyme

Money

If it ain't about money
I will pass
Cause I'm shooting for that money
Straight cash
My money coming
Like my car goes fast
I'm still spending money
That I had in the past
I used to sleep on money
Now I'm
Using Q-tips to get
The money out my head
I'm sleeping with $20's
'Cause $20's are in my bed
But I'm cheating on $20's
'Cause mo' money in my bed
I spend to make
Give to take
If we played chicken for money
I'll never hit the brake
This ain't a video
My money ain't fake
Thanks again to the people
Who made the money I make
Money makes money
That's why I got it
I got it in the bank
And I keep it in my wallet
Wear four rubber-bands
To hold it in my pocket
I got money in me
Like electric in socket
My pants, like
My pockets run deep
My money like me
Will never sleep

Addicted to the Game

I'm killing y'all
I'm MC Henchman
I can flow all day
I don't need an intermission
I'm in this game
Like a ….knife in the kitchen
Hip-Hop is my new
Found addiction...
...And I'ma
Addict
Lines come automatic
I don't use manuals
Y'all can have it
Being good
Is my good habit
I'm addicted to the game
I don't need no fame
Just want you to hear the word rap
And think of my name
When the audience claps
I want to be the blame
I'm climbing the staircase
Try to go to the hall of fame
Cause I'm moving in the game
Like it was my own house
Putting pictures in the frames
Of me and my spouse
Me and my mic
Me in the house
I love this game
Like I love the south

I Stay Myself

That's the opposite of troublesome
Quiet boy
But I still get in trouble some
Beef with me on the mic
You'll be in some trouble son
I'll spit something crazy stupid
'Cause I know you're dumb
And I know
I ain't the only one
Only in my teens
Rhyming like I'm 21
I get it popping on the mic
Like some bubble gum
Eat y'all other rappers alive
...YUM, YUM
I ain't the best rapper yet
But I'm close to the one
I'll be the #1 seller
When my album ain't close to done
The table is set
And I'm ready to run
Ain't nobody hotter than me
under the sun
And I'm holding that spot
#1
Cause I'm nice with a mic
Like a sniper with a gun
Never say you never seen a star
Cause you looking at one
But I want to be that galaxy
Case you can always look past a star I got me one

With 1 Parent At Home

Feel like I'm always defending
Like I'm play zone
When he on his own
Just like a king can't be a king
Without a throne
But on the other hand
My weak father made me strong
He taught me without teaching me
Cause I grew up ONLY
Gotta keep pushin'
Cause the doors ain't open for me
Gotta rap
Cause a job ain't working for me
Can't stop
That's the ONLY thing going for me
And if he clap
That's the ONLY way my father supported me
Yep I'm in this world alone
1 mom, 1 fam.
1 microphone
1 life to live
With 1 parent at home

Shoes

I don't wear Van's
Like Astro
I wear blue Jays
Cause of my pigeon toe
I'm talking Jordan's
If you didn't know
They Blue like my dog Pluto
My shoes
Whiter than every president
Got so many shoes
A shoe box is my residence
My shoes fly
Like they're heaven sent
Being fly, I'm guilty
Charged for walking, I'm innocent
I'm jay walking
With no lights around
Jays on my feet
Like dogs in a pound
I holla what's up
They say you and look down
To see best shoes out around town.

Atasia Burwell

.

Outside Looking In

Uncontained while trapped in a box
Nowhere to run nowhere to hide
New ego
Old pride
That one of a kind voluptuous pride
Years of keeping it is
Inspirational sit-ins
Bringing back memories full of sin
Hate misery and deceit pushing in
Pain loneliness and love showing out
Pushed aside brushed off and cast away
Outside looking in but yet
They can't
Judge me
Oppressed and depressed
Not to mention repressed and stressed
Drama and gossip
Time for a change
A stuck up pretty girl in a hardcore
Gang scene
Teen love measuring
Out to be love pain
Pain to shame I shame to anger
Anger to exclusions exclusion from change
Change to loneliness
Contained in a box
Stressed and depressed
No one to talk to
No one to comprehend where I been
But yet I remain free
Now fantastic
You outside looking in
Tell me
Is that how you seen it?

How Do I Deal

Being the victim
Of so many mistakes,
You breathe.
Insecure and unstable;
Being the root of so many
Problems
You become an image of
Preconceived ideas,
Then you realize
All those so called mistakes
Are no more than
Unforgettable sins.
Losing trust in life
Crying yourself to sleep at night
Losing faith in God and those around you
At the age of thirteen experiencing the touch
Some women only dream of
At the age of 17 realizing it was never a dream
But a nightmare
Someone I thought cared
Shared nothing but unwanted attention
Never in my life did I expect this could happen to me
The unreal is completely real
So I ask you
How do I deal?

Nykema Carr

Life

Life is like art
Drawn by the Man,
the Man called God,
Allah
or Yaweh
who gave us
life to breathe, walk, feel
taste, talk, think, create
and repopulate on this
beautiful planet called
Earth
every 5,000 years.
An Earth which we are destroying
with pollution, poachers and hunters
decreasing the
number of animals
to extinction
and yet we sit back watch each other
murder, kill, slaughter,
manipulate, lie, steal,
draining out own numbers
while the Devil himself
sits back and watches
the show
the souls of our brothers & sisters
God's children also sinners through the
hands of wrath called Satan
and become his slaves

Tiffany Carson

I am 15 years old I was raised in Durham, North Carolina. The inspiration for my poetry comes from my deepest innermost feelings. I keep a lot of things hidden inside. I use poetry as a way to express what I feel. Most of my poems are about my relationships, the ups and downs of being in love. When you're in love you face many emotions that weigh heavily upon you. Also, being at a young age it's hard to deal with unstable feelings that you can't control. Poetry is my way to truly express my thoughts to clear my mind.

"Being in Love is giving someone the Chance to destroy you, but trusting them not to" -Anonymous

7-29-07

Why is this happening to me
Words around me that I can't see
I am in a fairy tale called make believe
Hurting surrounds the insides of me
An internal pain nobody can see
Silent tears, alone in a crowded room
Wondering how long will this last
Can't continue thinking of the past
Live life with no regrets
Even-though I am highly upset
Pray on bittersweet revenge
Forgetting my Christian ways
Knowing only Jesus saves
How much more can a person take
Before he or she escapes
But not wanting to be alone
Wishing an angel could call my phone
Listening to my heart
Which is scattered in pieces
To fragile
To regain or sustained
A stable mind
I hate this moment in time
Not able to fast forward or rewind
Good things come to those who wait
How long do I stand in line?
Before I see what's mine
Trying to stand tall,
All but my conscience falls
Needing or wanting what is not there
Realizing I deserve better
Knowing this love may not last forever

Just Pleased With Me

Some people might see me as cocky or conceited
But trust me
You're misled
By your judgment of me
As a person that you see.
BUT
I guarantee I don't care
So don't dare to make me cry
Or break me into what you see
A false assumption
You are just in an Assumption of nothing
Mind your business
Just dismiss this (ME) out of your mind
I'm too many words that can't be defined
Yes I think I'm Fine
It's high self-esteem that empowers me as a person
A strong woman
I learned from my mother
I heard from father
I saw from my brother
How a woman should be treated
The man should please the woman
And acknowledge her strength
Because she's beautiful not sexy
So let me say
I don't need a man to make me understand
The true meaning of happy.
Just this high self-esteem
That empowers the insides of me
And my smile will show that
I am beautiful!
From inside to out
Without a doubt
I'm not cocky or conceited
Just pleased with me!

In an Anxious State of Mind

In an anxious state of mind
I am gathering thoughts we used to share
Me saying "Yes" when I meant No
Wanting something extremely bad
That I didn't need
Not knowing... what now is the Obvious
Feeling like it was a mistake that I want to retake
Fantasies of you being here
When I know that won't happen
Letting go when I want to hold close

Being confused about if I was used
Not knowing if I took the wrong path
And where I will end up
Trusting God is having faith
The easiest to say, but hardest to do
Everyday when I am in my own space
Trapped in between four walls
Daydreams of you accompany me
Looking at your pictures fills my eyes
Looking at our letters makes me cry
Seeing your name jump starts my heart

Anxiety builds wanting you back
Anxiety fades. The thought of you with another girl
Sadness overpowers my anxious feelings
Wondering if you think of me.... they way I think of you
When all I see is that you have moved on
But everything is not like it seems...you may think of me
I'll never know.

You're not my boyfriend
But you still have my heart
Not knowing to finish this book
Or keep striving to the very end

My mind is in a daze over decisions I have already made
Consequences that have taken place
Too late to erase what's said and done
But not wanting it to be over
Thinking I have failed my mission to you
I just don't know what to do...in an anxious state of mind

Mental Space.. ?.. and a Pause.. Undefined

Try to find mental space,
By saying Goodbye
Left alone to cry
Water is still upon my eyes
Facing your back
Pain in my heart attack
Need this feeling to go
I don't know if it's leaving or building stronger
Please just go
Ummm maybe no
Too many memories to fade under snow
Our history could be pages to a book
A step in life we both took
But the aftermath is now a story on your own
Figuring out how you stop feeling alone
Your other-half is gone
Believing everything you once had
Was the truth But a lie
A promise never kept
Showing you were willing to forget
Saying No then Yes
I mean Yes but No
Indecisive decisions you took on accident
But everything happens for a reason
That's a fact
What doesn't kill you makes you stronger
Is a quote
That you take as a mental note
Wise people say
If you love someone let them go, if they come back then you know
its true love,
Letting go is hard
But a task that must be done
To find out was he a waste of a time
Or the imperfect one that completes your soul
Only god knows
Why is this so hard
Something easy to fall into
But difficult to escape
Running images in my mind
Sentences never finished
Arguments never solved
Now all this has to dissolve
Still a ? and a Pause

Brandon Carver

Life

A man without friends only lives for revenge,
life is dream, making everything seem real,
why live the American dream, turns out it's really a scheme,
to kill. No matter how hard life makes you try,
you're always going to fly high, just put your mind to it,
don't complain, don't freak out or go insane, just be real,
making a good life is so cheap, its almost a steal. Blood, sweat and
tears, go into the elixir that vanquishes all your fears, pain is the
thing that makes joy what it is, worn out faces, worn out places,
dreams crushed and torn, complaining will screw you from when
you're born, live your life by the code your sworn, don't let anger
adorn your life, don't live it with strife, street life will send you
under the knife, or into the grave, don't be an idiot, don't try to be
brave, resurrect the dreams you buried alive, let your brain buzz
like a beehive, we've all got to die, isn't any use to cry, just say
your goodbyes, whisper a prayer, and get on with it, take it from
me, choose your choices wisely, don't hesitate, we're all waiting on
you, remember, life is a simulation, and life will always rely on
assimilation.

Dajanelle Davis

All Aboard

Line, Step
Line, Step
Line, Step
Line, Step

Red like Rudolf
But not from happy
Drip drop o'so slow but
Let's make this snappy
First 5, now 4
This feels so crappy

The door first cracked
But now wide open
That light so bright
Just keep on goin'

No wait- come back
It's too far and distant
I don't want you to go
I think you should miss it

Chugga, chugga choo choo
Closer closer to that point when we exposed her

No more, no more of this can I take
Too fast that past
Please not at this rate

Just wait, just wait
12 months same date.

Andrea Daye

My name is Andrea Daye. Writing poetry is a hobby of mine. I love to write anytime, no matter how I feel. I write poetry to release just about everything I feel. In my opinion, poetry is the key to peace.

Broken

On the ground I lay...
Lay face down,
Back open...
Soul broken...
Soul taken...
Are you done yet?
A trip turned into a nightmare,
Back broken...
Soul broken...
Are you done yet?
Tears flowing...
But that doesn't slow you
As you force-
Soul taken...
Force yourself between my immature features
Soul broken...
My immature mind as I look behind
But daddy I'll be fine...
Back open...
Soul broken...
Soul taken...
He only took my mind
Made me better-
Soul taken...
Now I'm rebuilding...

"There Comes a Time When Silence is Betrayal"
-MLK Jr.

Betrayal is silence, when the time comes
The time is everyday though
Where I aspire to show what's truly on my mind
I'm shot down with cold eyes
Cutting into my soul
Drenching the blood from thoughts
They flow
Flow down my spine,
That holds me up so strong
But if it's so strong,
What's holding me back?
Betrayal is silence when the time comes...
Silence...
Silence.

Brandon Easter

When

I see the destruction around me.

Lives gone.
Homes obliterated.

As the fire rains down
I ask,

Shall we be born anew?
When
Shall we be saved
from our sins?
When
Will salvation come?

Gazing

I gaze into the sky
To find what was
Lost to me;
That which was
Forgotten among men,
Invisible to all but
The higher power;

My soul.

Chandell

Hi, my name is Chandell. I am 16 years old; I have lived in East Durham for the past 5 years. I like it here I have made some friends, and some of them I have lost. I have a few hobbies that I like to do and one of them is writing poetry, and I write my poems dealing with the way I feel, and the things that I am going through at the time or have gone through. So I hope that you can either relate to them or enjoy what I have to say about things.

To Say

To say that I still care about you
Is sometimes hard to say
Because you make it hard for me
To even still want to try to care
Over and over again but after a while
I am just like forget it all together
I am through with it leave me alone
But after a while I still care bout you
With all my heart no matter what happens
You know I will always care about you
So stop making it hard for me ….

Message

Give it life
Give it hope
That one day he or she could be the pope
Give it a dream
Give it possibilities
That he or she could be like you and me
If it's a dream you want
Then a dream you shall get
As long as there's not to much to bear
Give it your heart, mind, body and soul
Not much to sweat
And you just might reach your goal
In return a world of possibilities
That you would never expect
That would be

Question

When it is time to let go
Of everything or everyone
Release yourself
From your life,
but do you still
You still hold onto
that special person
or do you
Let them go also

Hope

Hope isn't something that
Is given to you
Instead it's
Something that can be given
But taken away as easy as
It was given
By not having
Anything or anyone to believe in
Or have hope for them,
You should...
So do have
Hope or not ???

Yes

If it's a journey you want
Then a journey you shall get but
Be smart, not too quick

Gossip

Talking smack so this is what you will get
Girls run their mouths but nothing
Comes out but chit-chatter coming
From someone who is just a scared to
Say to your face because they might get spattered
From the sight of your fist in their face so if
You are that type of person then just know be warned
That if you talk it then you better backs it up
Cause if you don't you will get smacked up

Woman

Wonderfully loving
Outgoing, with love
Motherhood she willingly enters.
Angel she is to all. She is wanted,
Needed- some people fear to say.

Loved One

Spending time with family
Is a great thing; seeing loved
Ones you haven't seen.

But
Someone is missing.

What happened, no one is willing to say.
So you have no choice but to find out from
Someone else and that is not
The way that you wanted to find out the family secret.

That someone passed away.
You can't believe what you just heard.
You say "It's not true. You're lying to me".
But you know in your heart of hearts
That they are not lying to you, so what
Is there to do, but say

       Sorry…….

Slow and deep
To you

Not Saying Goodbye

With love,
One can leave you feeling like you have lost
Your best friend, the person whom
You trust with your life the person you
Talked to when you were going through a
Tough time in your life, when there was no
One else who you could trust.

So what do you when your love goes away?
Start blaming yourself for the
Death of your love, your best friend.
Find yourself thinking about the good
Times and the bad you may have had?
Now that they are gone, you can't talk
To them anymore face to face and the
Things that you may have never got to say go unsaid
Like your chance to apologize
For the words that stung so hard.
Would they have forgiven you?

But the thing that hurts the most
Was and is not having the chance to say the word

Goodbye

He

There is no one as blind as the man who will not see
Whether it's about his past or the present
He wishes to see beyond all the lies and betrayal
He never yells, to let out all the pain
that he's held onto his whole life,
Kept buried inside
Hidden from all
Even when
His true love could tell what he was feeling
And how bad he was hurting from it all…..

That Place

Have you been to a place where it feels so right to you
To be there in total peace and quiet,
Where no one can bother you
Or ask for this or that…..
A place that is …
Meant for you and no one else
Even though you want to share this wonderful feeling
Of finding yourself, but you are trapped by the choice to let
Yourself free of all the hurt and anguish that you have
Within you..

Peggy Ann

I cannot go to school today
Said little Peggy Ann McKay
Because I couldn't find my shoe
My cell phone broke in half last night
I had a dentist appointment at 3:00
What's that? What's that you say?
You say today is...... Saturday?
Goodbye, I am going out to play.

Love

To be in love, or to feel in love
What's the difference?
Can you even tell
if there is one at all
or is it a trick of the mind
They are both dealing with the same word "love"
Which is real and which is fake
do you just say It without any remorse
for that person feelings
or Is it something you say only at special occasions?
Or when you want that person say it right back
with the same emotion that you said it to
Them in...

Really Now

For someone that hasn't seen you in
Years and to act like a damn fool when
They do see you, how do you think that would
Would make you feel like "man what the hell is wrong with you?"
Maybe I shouldn't have come here to see you after all
These years of not seeing me, you as well
That was a very big mistake after all
Yeah, yeah, yeah you say that you that you love me
And not a second goes by that you don't think
About me come on now we both that's just a load of bull
And that it something that you think I want to here you say to
me

Tazjia Harris-Paiva

Absentee Daddy

88% of children in America
Have mommy and daddy
You see mommy is the daddy
'Cause daddy was a punk and ran
Away from what he made
But mommy stayed
She's great at multitasking
Gentle and firm at the same time
Taking both roles
So the absences of daddy doesn't
Hurt so bad
For daddy, mommy was a fiend
Nothing more than what was
Hot at the time
But time passed
And as time went by daddy
No longer wanted mommy
But by then the seed was already planted
To him that didn't make a difference
And when he left no one paid attention to him
Mommy had to have done something to make him feel out of
place
But no one realized that mommy was scared
Or did anyone care?
Didn't matter to mommy she was gonna do what she had to do
Mommy stayed
As I look forward
I see all that could happen
But as I look back
I see the weight of what
Everybody didn't do

George Hart

My Eyes

My Heart is racing.
My mind is chasing,
with thousands of thoughts.
Between Love and Hate.
Wondering how I could feel this way.
Feeling I'm in this tight spot.
Like I have a gun to my head.
Like I'm about to be shot,
by the bullet of this cold world.
Being told 'lies' from these people.
I feel like the world is against me.
I wish I could open my eyes,
so that people could see me.
Look into my eyes!
Can you see the real me?
I am just asking

With You

Wishing I could be with you
Every hour, minute, second
Of the day.
You make me feel good and you
Keep me smiling.
When we are together I am
Straight wilding.
I'm happy I'm with you,
I hope you can see.
I picture us in the future,
Just you and me.
I hope we can stay together.
Just you and me,
No matter what!
All I need you to do is
Just trust me.

Trapped

Trapped in this negative mind,
Feeling like the last in line.
Like the caboose on a train.
It really drives me insane;
Wondering will my mind ever change?
It works my mind when I feel like this.
Praying to the Lord
To help me with this.
If I could just make
A wish,
To change my mind,
To help me understand,
How I can be a better man.
Just help me.

Love

This word has four letters,
It can either kill you
Or make you better.
It has a lot of meaning.
It can make you feel good or bad.
Happy or sad.
Emotions fly high when it's said.
People can die over this four letter word.
This word can burn.
It can put you in another world,
Have you high off the feeling,
Or make you feel good.
But soon enough,
It will change your mood.
This four letter word could hurt you.
This word is called Love.

To Feel

I feel locked down,
With nowhere to go.
Like my freedom has been taken away.
Like I have lost my mind.
I feel like I'm in a mental lock down.
I feel like a puppet,
I just wish I could be set free.
I'm pouring my soul out.
Please just help me.
Set me free from this metal lock down.

Why?!?!

Why should I sit here and cry
A river of tears coming down my face?
My insides feel like their about to die.
I gave you my hearts and soul,
Now you want to up and go?
Why do you have to make me feel this way?
You have me feeling emotionless.
I gave you my heart,
You tore it apart.
I gave you my soul,
And you killed me slowly,
The thoughts in my mind
And now I'm going crazy.
All I'm asking is why?
Can you help me stop the tears
From falling down my face?

These Are My Feelings

These feelings run deep,
It makes my skin Creep.
It sounds like the music of my heart,
When it beats.
I get butterflies from this.
It's a feeling I hope not to miss.
I feel this when we kiss,
When we hug and smile
I feel like I have the love bug.
It has me smiling often.
I hope this feeling is real.
Could this feeling be the deal,
That could change my life?
These are my feelings!

Emotions

This is killing me.
I don't know what to do.
I'm tired of being hurt, cant you see?
I feel like my life is over.
I have lost everything in my life.
I feel like dying,
Just cut me with a knife.
My heart is beating really slow.
Could this be the end?
Is it my time to go?
My love didn't mean anything,
I guess you can go.
Just run out of my life,
And make me die slow.
I don't think I can love anymore.

Thoughts

I'm just sitting here thinking about you
You stay running through my mind all day
I can't wait till I touch your soft skin
Kiss your smooth lips
Whisper in your ear that I will never leave you
Hug you and feel your heart beat along with mine
I mean you got a nigga thinking about loving you
I'm not sayin that's a bad thing but to know that
You feel the same about me makes me so happy
I just hope that you don't up and leave a nigga
You're like the angel that looks over me
The air I breathe
You're the one I think about when I wake up and go to sleep
Could this be true love?

True Enough

I wish I could hold you, be with you -
Hold you in my arms and say I love you
I know you're going to be there for me
And I'm going to hold you down
Thank you for turning my frown upside down
I just wish that I could be there when you need me
You know you're the one
When you're running through my mind
Even when I'm asleep I'm dreaming about you
Can't stop to breathe without
Talking or speaking about you.
You're my angel that looks over me, proud that you 're my baby
Be happy that you're here, I'm proud to call you wifey
Can't stop thinking about you I think you might have me sprung
Your name runs through my mind all that can wait to talk to you
You put a smile on my face thinking about chillin' with you
You make me happy I wish I could get close to you

Life of a Trapstar

Standing on the block
Moving that weight
Trying to make sure
My family straight
Hoping five-o won't
Take me away
It's hard out here
Trying to make these bills
Cops patrolling
I got my finger on the steel
Watching me back 24/7
Praying on the block
I make it to heaven
Hoping life past won't come to my future
Of being locked up in prison
Almost got life messing with this bum
Back against the wall
Gun to my head
I thought this was done
Cops had the fifth
Pointed to my head
Put ya hands behind ya back
He said
Now I'm on parole 5 years under
When I get off
I'll probably do it all over

Brittany L. Henderson

Tears of Hope

Hope is like looking up at a beautiful star-filled sky
And just at that moment knowing that things will get better.
Hope can set your mind free
From the distress of what you think awaits.
Hope is like bursting into tears of joy
After a helpless time of failed inspirations
And achieved frustrations.
Hope is finally getting what you've
Been waiting ever so patiently for.
Hope can turn the worries of today,
Into the lifelong dreams of tomorrow.

Matthew James

"Yeah, that's great."

When one tastes the fruit of love they experience sensations unknown to the heart but home to the soul.

Everyday life passes me by, but I can't help to wonder, why? Why, everything I do, say, speak, or even see, doesn't make sense. I need you in my life, like the flower needs the sun; everyday that passes by I cry, dying just to see you smile or even speak a word towards me. Your voice is like the angels, gentle and sweet; like a delicate flower taken in the morning dew. I strive to reach the stars, so I can see your beautiful moonlight eyes shining as bright as the mind of an innocent. Interminable is your beauty, stretching across the heavens; never ending in the eyes of all those who look upon your face.

Doubt I've never seen your face, you remind me of the rose, glorious and notorious in all its wonders. Like a rose you are, but I myself am like the tree. Strong I stand, growing a new ring with the passing of age; weathering away with each tear I cry as the blade continues to pass through me. Truly, the last thing I want in these final times of life is to pass a message in the wind:

Every time I look at you, I can only catch a glimpse of your beautiful face, before I have to turn and look away. I-I want to say so much,...so much more than a two letter word, but I can barely manage to speak or even whisper the word "HI." Whenever I take that short glance; I always get to see the eyes of an angel with a smile so charming, it brings paradise to mine. I've never knew anyone who could speak to such a goddess as you; that's why I could have only dreamed of being with you.

I've always believed that life never worked out like you expected and that nothing and no one is perfect, but you in my eyes are. Three words describe how I feel about you, but for me it's always love at first sight. So I don't know if it's me or just an illusion; a struggle between mind over matter!

I've always been surrounded by love, but in all the time that I've been on this earth, I've never known the touch of true love, but only felt its presence. Someday a four letter word will be nothing more than just a word!

Every second that passes by, another piece of me dies, as another rises in the ashes. I continuously change everyday, but the love I have for you, will never change, nor be forgotten.

Your life in my eyes and that's what makes you perfect, and next to your beauty in my heart theirs no equal. I see life in your eyes and I hope you can see the love in mine. In the final words of the earth, all things in this world can't last forever; everything that has a beginning has an end and to forget those you love, is to have never loved at all.

I

Fallen from grace
Like an angel who has
Lost his wings;
My sky is clouded.
What was once blue
Is now just a mere
Shade of gray;
The storms begin to set in.
The light that once guided
Me through the day
Exists only as a shimmer;
The sun begins to set over the horizon.
It is now raining;
My life is in the dark.
Going on about nothing
I ramble in my own self-pity.
My heart has lost its feel
As it continues to cease its beat.
Time has stopped as death sets in
And the darkness consumes me.
The breath in my body
Returns to the wind; my body
Returns to the earth;
When I am found it
Will be eleven ribs counted,
For my love contains the twelfth.
The people surrounding me understand me not, for I am just a
leaf amongst the wind. Overlooked by all those who pass, a
diamond I am not for I will never shine. I am the flowing water
free and unrestricted in all acts. Time causes me no haste, for
where I am it doesn't exist.
To begin from the end means to go back to the beginning, but
not as in time but in start. What was always wrong was never
right?
-A whisper amongst the wind

Angel Tears

Crystal blue ice tears
From an angel that was told to never love
Destroyed by its hearts one true desire
Burning passionately inside like crimson red fire
Hidden away inside
Never to be heard seen
Or expressed by this
Angel full of rage and
Darkness.
The more and more the angel cried
The further the fire rises up
Burning stronger
Brighter with every
Tear cried
Until it couldn't
Be withheld.
But as the fire rises
So does the pain
Rage every night
Gazing at the moon
Crying crystal tears that reflect
The moons glorious light
Crystal blue burning fires
Frozen over with
Rushing waters of rage
Denied for what it wants the most.
Every tear falling
Clouds causing darkness
Rain of anger
Rage falls to the place
Where it's hearts burning desire
Lies waiting
Watching its pain
And destruction caused
By an angels tears.
Whose tears
Caused by the loss of
The purity of a kiss
The kiss of true love
From the one
Its heart desires the most
The one who is
Bound to earth
By life.

Only death will
Lift the bound
Unlocking the angels fire
Extinguishing it with
The kiss of true love
But to bring death
To the thing it loves the most
Is to destroy what it desires the most
To love.
But if love is the
Obsession in its heart
And it can over power the rage
And hatred against all others
The angel will have nothing
To worry about.
But if darkness
Conquers light
Then what's the purpose
Of love if the earth is covered
In darkness and chaos
Spreading throughout the world
With every tear cried
Giving the angel will have no need
To cry.

Freefall Fall

My wings are clipped	attract
Life rises up to met me	nouns
As I fall to met death	shutter
Lifeless in my peril	impact
The blade didn't	thunder
Cut deep enough	rain
My thoughts	lightning
Have been	sound
Stricken	murder
I	death
Just couldn't take it any	fault
More time I had left two	flaw
Ladder too climbed down	draw
The thoughts that pass us by	tragic
As we look toward the inside	fall
To see the people inside	lost
Hide what can't be	control
Seen behind	fear
Closed	emotion
Doors	thoughts
Tied	flashbacks
Head to toe	false
Mind to body	images
Yin to yang	logic
Unleashed in a fury each flurry	turned
Incognito of the facts shredded	down
Covering their tracks hearts [end]	drowned

The Jump

Caught in the downfall of my falling action
Time is of the essence;
Frozen in space with no form
Between loss and existence
It is there for none.
Darkness covers the light
As day stays the night in a
Never-ending cycle.
We are to run and jump the fence that bounds us from our
freedom.
Between the boundaries of blood and water,
Survival is the thickest
Right and wrong don't exist in a world where needs aren't met
Fist is to lightning as blade is to sword
Neither born with man, but gained through experience
In life's many faces we are just pawns in another mans gain.
Black and white is all they see; color-blind like the dogs they
represent.
Names are among the common
Never repeating nor terminating;
Their thoughts are of the irrational ones.
We are the devils of sin,
Our lust, gluttony, greed, sloth, wrath, envy, and pride are our
virtues.
We are the angels of holy,
Our chastity, temperance, diligence, patience, kindness and
humility are our virtues
We are the balance that keeps the world;
Never turning the page,
Just flipping the script.

Orb Persona

The flames of love
Are said to burn
Hotter
And
Deeper
Than hell,
But I feel nothing.
All I see is pure emptiness,
Like the entrance into your heart;
Flooded by the tears of a predestined sorrow.
Rejoice in your malice.
For rage is a minor reflection of my self-pitying soul
Torn from the inside out
Never feeling the pain,
Because worlds collide when Titans meet.
Darkness falls to light and light to day.
Time is drowned in haste of fear
As I stand frozen
On looking your departure.
I've lost my composure,
My dear goddess Isis,
You've brought me to my knee.
Oceans divided by the masses-
Resistance is my tragic flaw…..

War's Peace

Walking in the shadow without a doubt of fear
Arising from battle in the blood of the enemy
Red horse carries war and the white famine
Lusting for the desire to find that one
Offering life in one hand and death in the other
Viewing death as the only answer to the prison called life
Eternally striving to reach the love that is you
Prices are paid to have what won't come
Empires are built on what will never last
Acquiring this means to give up all that you love
Cause of death and destruction of those in the world
Ending all life to gain what is peace
Justifying a feeling without origin
Overcoming the things necessary to express it
Yet we always have to understand it or joy
Following a path that comes with no choice
Acting upon that like a wind with no direction
Thriving on a string with no faith
Each word represents a struggle but none like that is fate
We walk in war every time you underestimate the power of those
who influence you. Time stops as the heart beats in the rhythm
of love or fear of perishing in the battle.
We all come together in a time of peace only to end it in tragedy
or the fate of another falling nation struggling to understand the
meaning of the words.

I/AM

Like the wind
I never have to speak a word
My presence will always be known.
I'm alone in the world
Like all those who have been
Forgotten.
No one sees my pain
Nor can they feel my sorrow.
Empty is my heart
For there is no one who
Could fill it
No one who
Loves me or
Even sees me.
Death is
My only comfort
Blood is
The oath I
Live by
My life is
Mine and
Only mine to
Take.
I've made my vow
A pact I now hold
With my soul
To rise from the valley
And fear the shadows
No more.
To sleep in
The pits
Embrace the flames
Of the lake
Flowing through
The body
Giving life
To the impulse.
One moment
Rain or shine
This is the time
Of the final line
Of my kind.
I fight for you not
You live to see me suffer

I do not.
You can't describe something
By saying what it is
Not.
I am the calm wind
Passing with the breeze
The still river
Continually flowing
The timid earth
Covered in disillusion
The tempting fire
Raging in an inferno
The everlasting darkness
Embracing the abyss
The shining light
Guiding in the mist
I am one of many forms
Of life
And one of the mere image
Of death.

In the Madness

Why my mind will never stop thinking about you, I will never know. Maybe this confession letter will set my mind free of the soul that brought it to be in a state where it's imprisoned in an eternal flee...
Ha ha haha ha ha haaa...
For I write of you like a man without sanity. The love
I have for you burns deeper than the madness that
Drives me to confess these futile thoughts that
Run through my mind as I run out of time
Like this poem with an endless flow of rhymes, only
Stopping when this paper runs out of lines, or the
Darkness finally engulfs my mind making this
My final line.
The words I say could never equal the words I
Write, for my voice is only but a fragment of
My real thoughts, which are my words.
When I hear your voice, it's like a constant
Reminder of the pain that is you.
The one thing in this world I wish I could
Have, the only thing I would
Give my life for to save, you will
Never understand these feelings
I have. You make me mad every
Time you're sad. For I could be
The one to make you glad, but
Realize this thought isn't the one
About you, but about me because
You're the one that completes me
And take my thoughts to heart.
These thoughts are my unspoken words
Of truth like the love I express
When I look into your eyes and never
Speak the words I want to say
Leaving myself empty as a field without
A flower or a man without a soul
Trying to find his place in a world
That won't accept him and a life that
He never wanted
Taking a toll and
Paying a fee for
The mere plea of
Being set free.

You are my peace, joy, life, and love, it is you that completes me and makes me whole. Without you this earth is another hell. Purgatory is the prison binding me to this earth as a dream catcher trapping lost souls with its infinite lies and truth. Are you real or just another dream made up in the mind of a mad man?

Jasmine Joyner

To Exists

The struggle for existence ties
In with the survival of the most fit
A constant battle between hustlers
And those that are legit
Hustlers who are just scraping by
sellin' crack, gettin' paid, smokin' weed,
then die
Against the upstanding, legit citizens
who are creating a never-ending chain
of generations passing judgments,
long after our freedom-bell rang
They continue to turn up their noses
implying superiority
will there ever be equality
for this not so minor minority?

Tyrell Kejuan Knighton

The Witness in the Court

I charge you,
First degree murder,
Second degree murder too,
For this crime,
That you've been accused of too,
Your sentence,
Will be life,
Cause you follow a life of crime,
Do you have anything else to say to the court?
To prove that you're innocent and your not
lying,
The Defense said no,
But his Witness said yes,
Now everybody's looking at the Witness,
Like he's crazy too,
And then the Judge spoke out and said,
Wait I wasn't talking to you,
And then the witness said to the Judge,
Let me explain the truth,
I am the murderer,
Not my friend,
And then the defense got up and said,
I told you man,
Not to get up and try to save me,
And then the Witness spoke out to the Defense,
Saying,
Please forgive me,
But I can't live a lie,
And now both the Defense and the Witness are crying,
And now everybody can't believe
what they just heard came out the
Witness's mouth,
And since the court and the Judge heard,
What the Witness had to say,
The Judge said to the Witness,
What do you Plea?

Help Me

Help me be the person that I should be,
help me believe the power that's inside of me,
help me out of this tunnel,
for I have scene the struggle,
help me for you said peace be still,
for forgiveness is the key,
that will set you free,
in the time of need,
Just please help me

What if I Told You

What if I told you I love you?
what if I told you what I said was wrong?
what if I told you and told you again,
what if I told you and said I was wrong?
what if I told you I heard you and you said ok,
what if I told you?
will I see you the next day?
or will you just fade away.

I Am an Eagle

I am an Eagle,
An Eagle that can fly,
An Eagle that never gives up and dies,
Pay attention to me,
Because you will see that there is an Eagle in me.
You may see me mad at certain times,
It's just because I was doing bad at that certain time,
I know I have a friend
When I am in need of a hand.

Mold Me

Mold Me
Mold me to be the best,
mold me to success,
mold me but don't keep me away from my nest,
each day is a test,
so mold me to pass that test,
Mold me with knowledge,
instead of using me like a market,
mold me like a king,
or if you're a women mold her like a queen,
Mold me and just show off my being,
to let everyone know now,
that you're not going easily down.

Pain Pain

Pain pain,
it's the same,
as my heart proclaims,
as you see,
the pain in my heart will always have a beat,
yes it hurts,
but you won't see,
the pain that I have in my heart,
that's inside of me,
it's no game,
but it always feels the same to me,
for the days have passed,
and the pain I have kept in my heart,
has now proclaimed,
pain, pain,
it still feels the same.

I Use to be a Champ

I use to be a champ,
until I gave up,
and now I found out I need to get back up,
cause I can't just seat on the blessing that I have,
now I see light and the light is bright,
so I got to fight,
cause the day is almost over,
and I got to stay alive,
for my time is now,
it's time,
for me to rise,
to be the champ that I am,
it's a blessing,
so now you know my confession

I Feel

I feel down,
putting my head down,
don't know what to do,
crying,
yelling,
on my knees now,
keeping my mind on you,
praying,
saying,
forgive me Lord too,
for what I have done,
was not an act of you,
Then I will stand up and feel better,
but then I felt another test coming thought,
by God,
And I ask why,
why me,
and he said,
why not you,
and I said I feel you,
But why has thou chosen me,
and he said I feel you,
but why not choose you,
then I felt confused.

Beautiful

You're attractive in so many ways
All the way down from your face to your feet
You're cute and beautiful and smart too
Don't let anyone tell you you're not cool
Cause in my eyes I see more than just beauty
I see an intelligent girl full of dreams
And I know that you will succeed.

Even Though

Even though you're gone
I still feel your presence here
My life changed
I never really knew how much you meant to me
Until the end of the time came
And took you away from me
Now it's a whole new beginning
I have to take on the world all on my own
Starting back over; it's so hard cause
Without you
How will I start?
And how will I end?
I wish I would have known
That this was going to happen
But I know if I did
You would let it be
You were right no one could stop your destiny

No Mask

Let them only see the real side of me
Not the person that hides in my heart that fears and weeps
Not that side that is doubtful of itself and not unique
Let them see how down to earth I can be
Let them see my love that is unconditional and unique in every way
Let them see that I wear no mask

What Happened?

What happened to the girl that I used to know?
The one that used to talk to me
Even though
She had a boyfriend
She just needs to know
She still has the friend in me (oh)
Why you must act like you don't know me
Is your boy doing something
That he shouldn't be doing?
Girl, please talk to me
Cause that's what you used to do
When we were all close and cool
Don't act all shy
Cause you see me coming
Oh, oh
Baby why?
Why?
Why you must act like that?
Knowing that you don't love him
Why, why
You acting like That?
What happened to the girl I used to know?

Young Pac Kejuan

Everything you heard is false my brothers and sisters
If you're fed up don't give up, keep your head up and don't let up
We have to start making changes because the same old things aren't working
We were robbed of our history; they were so wrong for keeping us away from learning
I read that the classes don't exist anymore
But from what I see there is rich at the top, and poor at the lowest
Never Ignorant Getting Goals Accomplished that's the new meaning of the word nigga,
New meaning of black to brown white to peach, yellow to mix
But judge not on their color, but by their action, and their character
It's your time now so get up make a difference like Dr. King and Malcolm X and Rosa Parks did
No more pledging to this so called Home of the free, cause that's just a story but they force us to Pledge cause it's the law. It don't apply to me and my brothers and sisters of this country
So please don't tell me we live in equality- Lady Liberty isn't talking for us,
Lady Liberty, plead the fifth, now it's time to stand up and start making changes.

S on My Chest

Check out the S on my chest
It's hotter than the sun
Splat
Here I go
With another one
I'm gonna keep it new
While you keep it old
I'm not talking too fast
You're just listening too slow
I'm not losing
I refuse to
Some body parts have meanings
Let me explain
This figure means Screw you
So much money on my mind
Really that's all I could remember
Haters are always hating
From part time to time
Cause I'm
Fresh as a hustle
Yeah
Check out what I got
Looking for the baby momma
But found two cops
You're looking at the baby
Now he's a soldier
But those cops shot the baby momma
I was too young to save her
Call 9-1-1
Then Bush answered
He said sorry I don't help poor black ghetto strangers
So now the soldier writes his anger out on a paper
Catch me on TV on the news 24\7 of every hour
The S on my chest is so its stands for Stress and Super
Tell me what you want
I give you what you need
Lights
Camera
Action
Now you're famous and it's all because of me
One person talks hard
The others want beef
I give it both to them all
My level is harder than Supreme

Watch and I bet
I put you both down
Under 6 ft
Underneath the ground
I'm so hot
I'm so fly
I'm gonna keep it straight with ya
I don't need to lie
I use to think I wasn't going to make it
But really I wasn't thinking straight
Cause all I could remember was baby mama
Cause I had the S for Stress on my chest

Death Door KEY

When I was little,
I never really knew,
What was death,
But as I grow in life,
I now know what death is,
Death is a key, locking a door,
Death is the meaning of loss,
And no more,
Death is the beginning of the end,
For each piece of death,
It's always another piece,
Always adding in,
Death is a description,
Of loss and peace,
Cause when someone dies,
They rest in peace,
And there is no way you can unlock the door,
Cause there's no key
For the death door.

Life

Yeah I am different
Different from the rest of them
To the end of time
The period between birth and the present time
While there's life, there's hope
An animation and energy in action
History is then made up
Into a document
That determines your life
Cause you made a right or wrong action
That matters
Become ideas
Then the new technology is invented
Counting down
To that day comes
And I become finished
A system of capability of operating of learning
Some have a probability of failure
But to me 100 percent success
In my book
If they just stay and get that degree
Make that paper
But look the more you make
You're cutting down trees
But yeah I understand
We do the craziest things
To try and to become rich
But I ain't those trees
I ain't going to let you put me down
I refuse to let such
Eagerness take me out

Princess Langhorne

Breakups

Breakups are never easy,
So this poem may come of as cheesy.
We were friends but we wanted the next level,
But temptation can be a devil

We wanted more, but when we
Took the chance it didn't work out.
I'm not gonna even lie, when you asked me
Out I had my doubts;
Don't get me wrong, I always wish for the best
But overall you failed the test.

When we decided to be an "US" it got worse.
Seemed from that day forward it was a curse;
Some of us are just better off as friends
And we should have left it that way till the end,
But every time I think about you, us, it,
Your sex appeal gets to me; being friends without benefits
Can't be when it comes to you and me.

Sometimes I don't know when to say no,
But I always take the chance.
Say, "What the hell," and go wit the floe.
I mean, should I settle for less?
At that moment in time it seems best.

Because when I decide to take a new route
I end up regretting and forgetting my doubts.

Mr. Wonderful Isn't so Wonderful at All

Again I fell for his lies. Now I'm forced to hate and despise that four letter word and wash my ears to cure what I have heard. Again I chose to believe and to be left the only one grieving. I should have listened to myself the first time and chose not to fall but his luscious words and easy heart seemed to call. Every time I tried, he was like a drug; I couldn't let go and when I almost did, my feelings began to overflow.

You're right, it seems like I can't not be with you. You've become an instinct; I can't live without you so when I try leaving it becomes more like self doubt. Wonderful was the word I used to describe you; if only you knew about the late night when pain began to drive me insane. The disrespect was overbearing and your words were no longer caring. Your laugh became something I hated to hear and your hatred is something I feared as you rubbed off on me evil and mean attitudes which I used to get you back when lovin' you was something I began to lack.

Love is Pain

Love is pain,
Known to cause people to go insane
And ask the ultimate question "What did I gain?"
But for me,
Six more months
Is more than I can take.
And I don't want my love
for you to become fake.
I really believed we were a match
So willingly I became emotionally attached.
See, you disrespected me one too many times
And when I asked for some consideration
You acted as if it was a crime
I guess it's wrong for me to ask you to change
But I was unaware that your personality was short of range
I still love you so my feelings are still strong for you
But I can't continue this knowing you'll still treat me the way you
do
Your smart remarks and sometimes evil words broke my heart
So it's easier for me to see us apart
I'm not happy anymore
So it may time to close that door
Because you don't provide what I look for
The longer I take these breaks from you
The better it seems,
So it may be our destiny
To no longer be a team
I know I promise never to leave
But for your love to be,
How much longer do you want me to plea?

My Flaws and All

I want someone who loves me for me,
My flaws and all
Who will catch me when I fall,
Is that you?
If so, what is it that you do,
That makes you different from the rest?
If you love me, please confess...
I know when I have things on my mind
I become quiet and a bit boring
My moods change without warning
Sometimes I can be too much of a tease
But my goal is always to please
I want you to love
The wrong in me and the right
So that in the darkness
You become my light
So that you never give up on me
And realize I have the potential
To achieve everything I want to be
Love my attitude;
Jealous ways to my sarcastic remarks
So as our fire remains I still create that spark
Someone who understands
My secrets and my past
And will take on loving me
As their main task
Someone who won't continuously take me for granted
And realize I will take care of and nourish the love we planted
Yea I think I'm all that
And I might sometimes take it to the head
And sometimes my feelings become hard and unable to be read
Oh I'm more than your average wifey material
It balances my looks and internal
The biggest heart that you'll ever find
So my love easily blows minds.

Letting Go

A lot of emotions running in my head,
I still remember the words that you said-
Last time we talked- fighting and fussing
You screaming, me cussing
Now I'm just reminiscing
I wish we could have listened
Because our hearts never said no
So yes I'm still fighting to let go
I lie at night and think if you're thinking of me
Wishing you could look at yourself and see what I see
I can't help but think of what we could be
Hurting my heart seems to drive me insane
Tugging left and right on this love chain
Without you, parts of me are incomplete
Waiting for the next time we will meet
Do you feel lonely?
Baby, I want you to hold me
I miss you more than you could dream
And still you remain the drug that I fiend
Life seems so crazy it seems like I can't deal
Because without you, nothing seems real
I open my arms and wish you could occupy the place
But no one else seems to be able to fill the empty space...
I love you, and it's sad but it keeps getting stronger
And the more I try, the memories last longer.

In This I Believe (faith)

I believe soon he will come back to me
When I hear love songs I believe it is meant to be
Even though he is with a new chick every other week
I believe he will be back to make my heart weak
His heart became cold, in the street he fights
I believe he will still hold me late at night
In poems he relates to other girls
I believe I'm still his whole word
When he is alone in jail
I believe when I write him he will answer my mail
Even though he says she now has his heart
I believe we will never be apart
When I call and he doesn't answer the phone
I believe soon he will come back home
When he tells the girls the same words I used to love to hear
I believe in his heart I will always be near
3 years gone by and he tells me we are at the end
I still believe when I'm hurt the pain I feel he'll be there to mend
Back and forth we run back to each other
I will always believe I'm his only lover
Even when you say we're done
I believe your longing for me pours over and runs
I still believe I'll be the one you choose,
Therefore my faith in you I will never lose
Yeah for you I'll ride or die so I believe you're confused and
You're still my guy
And no longer will you make me cry
When it rains and I look out my window pane
I believe like me , us not together is driving you insane
I still believe I'll be the one you tell those words "I do"
And at the end I believe it will just be us two.

In the Beginning (dedicated to Dray)

In the beginning I never thought I would fall
That you would be the nigga I couldn't wait to call
It was a fantasy, you fulfilled my dreams
So it only seemed right for us to be a team
You made me believe in you
And in the end it would be just us two
I loved you so much
You caused that adrenaline rush
Then it happened, you turned to the streets
And so you learned to pack heat
The look in your eyes began to deceive
And it began hard for you to believe
Showing your love, you still tried
So I wanted to ride
But you began to get lost
And our relationship was the cost
Our arguments became fights on who's wrong and who's right
The breakups became often
Your heart, I tried to soften
Once you became cold and didn't want to go back
People not on your side becomes more of a fact
The good times became less
So you stopped to confess
Our love was anything but strong
About life for you was wrong
Still I tried to support
Especially when you went to court
We don't know if your life like this is forever
So you think its best for us not to be together
It cause so much pain
Hell ran over like rain
We held on as long as we could
If you asked me to do this again I don't know if I would
In this relationship things were taught
Trouble in paradise who would have thought
If you need me I'll still be here to provide my love and care
I don't blame you, I understand
These choices you didn't originally plan

I Give You My All (dedicated to Sean)

I give you my time
I give you my mind
I'll stop holding back
And give you the facts
I give you my heart
And believe we won't be apart
There's only one person I want to be with and that's you
And against everything in the world, it should just be us two
I give you my soul and my feelings become whole
You're everything I want and need; I'll strive to be
Because I want forever it to be just you and me
Even when things get rough and times change
I'll never judge you; my feelings will remain the same
You give new warmth in my heart,
A genuine wide smile on my face
So now my heart is where I keep you in place
When you "I love you" my heart gives in and stops
I put you above everything so you remain at the top
I'll give you a shoulder, where you can lean
And give you my honest opinion, when
You need it even if it sounds mean
Because I give you my all I had no choice but to fall
So now you have all of my trust
To get it back is a must
I'll give you that mutual feeling, that what we have is real
Never doubt the way that I feel
You're my boo, no choice but to spoil
You don't have to worry about me ill stay loyal
Because what we have seems so right
So giving you my all is no longer a fight

Picking Strawberries

The dude who "loved me", knew I would fall
and that every other dude would try and step up to the call;
the problem with that is that I don't know who's real
so I make wrong decisions on how to deal,
like picking strawberries it takes time and care
and at the end you realize nothing was fair.
I began harvesting from outside appearance
but they tasted bad,
so I went back to the ones I originally had.
You start off caring about each individual one, then you get tired,
but not doing what's expected will get executed or fired.
When I first chose (picking strawberries and becoming a woman)
I didn't realize it was a hard task...so as I smile and make
everyone else happy, I'm suffering under my mask.
You realize not everyone is going to be pleasing and there is
such a thing as too much teasing.
Pick them too early, they're bitter pick them too late, they're
rotten...but at the right time so sweet it will knock you off your
feet and just like a first kiss, can make you weak.
So I tried putting them in categories: big, tall, short, small, bitter
and sweet, and the ones that would cheat;
but not all strawberries fit into those categories, you have the
ones that are different, one of a kind so you don't mind spending
the extra time picking them gently.
You never realize the "NOT SO BAD ONES" until you find worse
and finding the right ones seem to be like a bad curse.
Let me remind you that new ones are steady coming and like a
dog goes after a bone you're steady running.
Not thinking it's a problem to sometimes add more and now it's
hard to tell what to look for.
So you wonder if it's worth all of this, for that moment of
bliss, to be able to hold on to the memory you will ultimately
miss.
Don't give up what you've learned; you will get tired of making
the wrong turn.
No more dipping in and out for the right taste, this time I'm
going to go at my own pace.

Yes I'm going to miss some good ones but I want to pick what's
right; the one who in the end will put up a fight.
Now I have to get over the issue of wanting perfection
and for now just go along with the connection.
Out here you got to be ruthless,
not every strawberry is needs to get picked

and is it so bad to withdraw when you want a taste or a lick.
See, you never knew picking strawberries was so hard just like in
a game you need to pick the right spade `
out from the deck of cards.
There is always a matter of temptation that seems to rise
and the good ones seem to be full of lies.
So finally I decide to go with the one that don't taste bad
and I cringe on the ones I could have had.
I'm here looking for the ones that are strong, long, durable and
built to last and I realize it might take time to fulfill this task.
hopefully patience isn't something I lack and I will continue to
grow and won't look back.

Ti'Ara Lyons

When Love Went Away

Poor pitiful me,
Tears I cry though you cannot see
I hide my emotions as well as my tears
Because they add to both my furies and fears
See love loved me
It's easy for me to say
Love loved me
But lust came and took me by the hand and led me away
And I had never planned to stay, I went back to love,
But when I went back to love loved pushed and loved shoved
See love had head about the time I spent with list and even
Though to me it amounted to dist
Love didn't want to hear about \what I had to say
Love didn't want me to leave but couldn't bear to stay
So I asked what could I do to make things right
Love told me that the deed was done and my low had reached a
New height
While leaving love wished me well
But it felt like I was being sentenced to hell

At this point I was so confused,
I had nowhere to run and nothing to lose
So I went to find lust and as you expected
Lust was looking for its own love
And time for me is now neglected

Lust and I shared multiple nights and many days
But I realized that it was the very first night that sealed my fate
This leaves me lonely and filled with hate

And even until this day I spit upon lust
And I praise love because love loved me
But lust came and took me by the hand
And led me away led me astray
And love, my love who once pledged never to leave did not stay
Yeah, my love went away
And now all I have is tears to cry
And nothing more to say.

Gena Mohwish

The purpose of life is far from blatant, perhaps because the purpose of life varies from person to person, thus making it more difficult to attain self-fulfillment, if it's even possible. It is my purpose to search for the truths in life, in thoughts, in lies. I aim towards deciphering the riddles of the simple complexities in life, ultimately realizing that it can seldom be done. I'm on a journey for truth and knowledge in any form whatsoever, to cease the aching inside. I face both unconcealed and clandestine verity, even perhaps at the same time. I am living a life in which the lines that divide sanity and insanity; abstract thoughts and logical thoughts; life and death; are blurred, or possibly just ignored.

Impending

In the wake of infinite contemplative sorrow
arises I,
the broken one.

They cannot be stopped,
these melancholic memories.
They cannot be stopped,
these violent tendencies.

I write like this sometimes,
because I feel small in comparison to the world.

But you don't even know this.
I can't tell you this.
I can't tell anyone this.
I can't tell anyone anything.
It's some kind of minor mental disorder, I think.

I can't find an appropriate ending for this so I'll just leave now.
This happens a lot in my life.

Sometimes,
I wish I felt inadequate
and didn't mind
sitting alone
in a corner,
where I really should be
anyway.

Gestated Fragments of Trivial Thoughts

My memory is dying, while my heart is trying to live. Trying to love. Always trying, but never succeeding. Now, it's come down not to whether or not I succeed, but if something happens. If something lies beneath the exterior. The only thing that is dividing this blank screen and myself is the array of scattered thoughts that I am working to unify. It's not working. I am meandering in life, but not in the good way. In the routine way. In the hollow way. But haven't I always been?

I want to be clever like you.
Not clever like me.

Not anymore.

Halcyon Delusions of an Ersatz Life

This is the time to concede
the peculiar notions of existence.
In a foolish attempt to gain a lucid perspective
of the conundrums this time around.
Without ever having solved the enigmas
from the last time around.

A perpetual state of autopilot operation
leads me to a perpetual state of
despondence.

And despite the ceaseless, countless revisions...
I'm still just the same,
only incognito.

One-sided Conversations With 'God'

Simple conversation starters are guaranteed to
turn into the most perplexing questions.
The most flawed logics.
The most misconstrued actions.
(Everything's perplexing, flawed, and ultimately misconstrued.)

The most (un)important questions asked are never answered.
Or even realized by the majority of the populace.

Blindfolded, defenseless, dubious.
It will never end.

A final letter,
no longer addressed to 'you'.
No longer addressed to anyone.
Just to keep you guessing.

Irrelevant Reiteration

Sometimes, our best attributes are latent. Other times, they are hated. But to be both is contradictory; again, a paradox applies to me. Will it ever cease? Perhaps, but that won't be the only thing that will cease. Everything will. Is that ramification even bearable?

To answer my own enigmatic question..........
Yes and no.
*Which is yet **another** paradox on its own.*

Here I am once again leaving secret messages everywhere in hope that you will discover and decipher them, wherever you may be. They know where you are, the ones that you spoke of with such hatred in your words. Yes, they know where you are, as if it wasn't blatant enough. But there's much more beneath that flawed logic, isn't there? I think you knew it, and now I do, too.
And I still sit, in disbelief of this reality that I wish was a dream, singing, "Now that I've decided not to stay, I can feel me start to fade away. Everything is back where it belongs; I will be beside you before long....." in the most feeble voice.

We'll see if it will suffice.

This (con)quest keeps leading me to desolate dead ends.
I expected it, though.
It is life, after all.

They Are

When you looked upon others,
With paradoxical eyes full of truth and distortion,
Did you see your own mortality?
Or were you blinded by everyone's oblivion?

You made it your point to be,
Not godly,
But godlike.

Depending on who you ask,
The task was either clever or unwise.
An achievement or a failure.
A revelatory event or a futile act.

But the unanticipated truth that all the critics and supporters fail
to realize,
Is that they are exactly like who they criticize and praise.
It's just not as clear as verity should be.

Rare Recurrences of Ancient Feelings

In the depths of my soul lies incomprehensible truths that are treasured for their beauty while I am suffering.
And it's these things, *the most inexplicable of things*, that make me believe I am truly blessed.

And the secrets of all this are only shared between two; or, in worse case scenario, the secrets are known only by one.
By only I.
But even if that turns out to be the case...I'll still have myself.
Which can either kill me or save me. But it's best to not know our fates before they occur, I suppose.
That leads to demise on its own.

Revelations or Lies?

Isn't it funny how two opposite actions can occur at once? I've been thinking a lot lately, while at the same time, not thinking at all. I guess some paradoxical ideas can be true. I'm just a lost cause who has found herself, but is misplaced in everyone else's eyes. I honestly don't think they're looking, though. I don't think they ever will. But what is there to look for? It's in front of them; can they not see the beauty of it all? It's pretty blatant, I believe. Unless I'm lying to myself, which, if the case, wouldn't be the first time. Retrospection along with introspection can be either malicious, or benevolent. Right now it's proving to be the former, which is unusual for me. But not completely unbelievable.

I'm waiting for my inevitable impending demise, because I've been waiting far too long for my life to begin.

042099

Catastrophe runs through the blood of the most
        innocent, leaving it forever tainted.
Our existence is our curse, and we are secretly
        doomed from birth.
Locked in a place where the river of
        solitude never runs dry.
Ulterior motives are exposed only
        after death as salvation is reached.
Mental capacities overload with angst.

Beneath the surface, contempt
        quietly transforms sanity into insanity.
Investigations take place, searching for ways to release
        emotions that are constantly suppressed
        indirectly by society and directly by medication.
Nothing but the sight of blood, misery,
        and death can appease the contempt now.
Extermination is the only option when the point of no return has
        been passed, and now there's no turning back.

A violent love that is shared between two.
Often complicated,
but never askew.

I am quite intrigued by my desire of simplicity in times of complexity.
But even more so by my desire of complexity in times of simplicity.

Does satisfaction not lie in my midst?
Maybe so,
but it certainly is hard to attain.

Loving You

Dark skies.
Countless lies.
Unbelievable highs.

Sickening lows.
Unhappily-ending shows.
Vicious blows.

Heart-wrenching fights.
Love soaring to new heights.
Hate taking many flights.

Sowing confusion.
Stirring emotions.
Stimulating lust.

Loving you.
Hating you.
Manipulating you.

All at the same time.

Philosophies of a Cynic

Time is deceptive.
Life is temporary.
Death is reliable.
They're my enemies.
They're my allies.

Each presents its own challenges.
But in the end, none of those things will fail me.
They keep their promises.

Good luck with naming other things that do.

I have an incurable illness that causes me write letters to those who cease to exist.
Have you noticed?
Sometimes I can't tell if I'm writing about someone real or imaginary.

Sometimes I can't tell if I'm real or imaginary.

I have little control over my senseless thoughts.

Sometimes I think too much.
Sometimes I think too little.
Sometimes I simply can't see the difference between the two
methods of thinking.

The voices in my head are becoming faint sounds, comparable to
those of a machine's demise.
The blinding lights of passing cars and streetlights fail to live up
to their reputation of actually being blinding.
The stifling summer air is suffocating me.
My thoughts are dissecting me.
My feelings are pestering me.

Fading in and out of consciousness, and losing track of time.
Pondering my life and my dreams, and speculating which is less
of a lie.
Failing horribly at envisioning what's going on in your head.

I just can't wait until nightfall, when I can be immersed into
darkness.
And forget my existence.
And yours.
And...hers.

Does the feeling of contrition haunt you as you're reading this?
I bet she won't ever speak of you in the same way I do.
Sometimes you're just so blind to the most beautiful things.
It's such a shame.

These words are only puzzles that perplex your mind. You'll never decipher the codes that hide inside. But you can follow the lines. Or you can dissect them. And then wonder why you chose to do the one you did.

I hope this eats you away.

That sunset has got you fooled, my love.
For its vibrant glow is as quixotic and deceptive as my words.
The searing summer heat devours us,
much like the desire that is shared between us.
Now, we have stolen time and grasp it tightly,
just to make sure this never ends.
Now, our hearts, minds, and souls intertwine.
But there's still a cryptic division somewhere.
I look into those flustered brown eyes that conceal your true identity.
And you look into mine, while uttering the most unanticipated words, in place of overused phrases.
"You're the most honest liar I know."
Ooh, does that mean I'm the best, too?

Where's the lovely location that all the clandestine emotions go?
I hope they don't die.
Set them free; it's not a sign of vulnerability.
Oh no, exposure is not the equivalent to vulnerability.
Your mind; your eyes; everyone's lies; have all shown a hint of inaccuracy.

But your heart has not.
Because it's the most honest thing in existence.
Solely because we don't have control over it.
Anything that is controlled, is instantaneously corrupted.
Minds. Words. Lives.

Let your heart sink into the depths of life,
but don't let it drown.
Let your soul fly into the never-ending sky,
but don't let it fall.
Let your thoughts plummet out of your mind,
but don't let them lie.

La Búsqueda

Dónde está mi corazón?
Dónde está mi alma?
Dónde están mis pensamientos?
Dónde está mi cuerpo?

Quiero buscarlos.
Quiero encontrarlos.

English Translation:

The Search

Where is my heart?
Where is my soul?
Where are my thoughts?
Where is my body?
I want to look for them.
I want to find them.

Miss Anthropist

I gather my thoughts.
Review them.
Revise them.
Then throw them away.

You gather me.
Review me.
Revise me.
Then throw me away.

Rosy Retrospection

Just keep concocting those lies with your idealistic words; you'll eventually create some that will even deceive yourself. Whisper what seems like sweet nothings in my ear. Who are you kidding? Who am *I* kidding? We both know that those same seemingly insignificant words create me, and will ultimately shatter my heart, my mind, my sanity, and all that I consist of. I'm in too much bliss to stop this now. Funny how people say ignorance is bliss, because so are you. Engulf yourself in me, and vice versa. Emotionally, that is. Or maybe physically. The line that separates the two is hazy in my eyes. And probably in yours, as well. I know that you no longer know why you're here. I don't even know why I'm welcoming you here again with my arms open wide, only for you. Always for you. It's not healthy, but it's better than sniffing cocaine from broken mirrors in dimly lit rooms to get the same effect. And which effect is being referred to here? Euphoria or destruction? Oh, I don't really have to limit myself to choosing one and spoiling the fun, do I? Give me the answers that I yearn for; I'm sick of implying dreadful things. Even though they're not implications, but rather facts. Oops, I forgot that you're far too delusional to see any facts that lie here, whether they're latent or exposed. Or maybe you're just too ignorant to notice them. Hmm...that sounds disturbingly familiar. More familiar than you. And even more familiar than who's looking back at me in the mirror. The dark circles under my eyes and pastel-colored skin seem to appear out of nowhere. Maybe they're here to symbolize my emptiness. In case you were wondering, I certainly am blaming you for it. Blaming you renders useless, though; I know you won't accept it. But that's okay. Just dispose of my accusations the very same way you dispose of the medication whose side-effects bear a striking resemblance to that of mine. Next time, try looking at the warning label on me that reads: *May cause corruption of the soul.* But I just thought I'd mention you, incase you started to worry that I had forgotten you. Never mind. Your vast ego won't even let you worry about that. Everyone already knows I won't ever forget you, anyway. It's inevitable. Kind of like how you will eventually forget me. Ah, did I just spoil the ending of this flawed story? Sorry, it's a force of habit.

And
I'm
still
waiting
for
that
near
~~death~~
life
experience
that
you
promised
to
give
me.

You claimed to have already given it to me, but I never saw it.
Are   you   lying,   or   am   I   just   blind?

How Many Pills Does it Take to Cause a Mild Case of Death?
I'm living a life that could easily be compared to a story submitted to a magazine by someone with the name 'Anonymous'.
A life in which I'm having to search my own vomit and stomach acid in hope of finding at least a few partially-dissolved, recently swallowed pills.
Just so I can have a little relief, and just so I can sleep without fear of not waking up in the morning.

I'm not going to be able to sleep tonight.

Cognitive Distortions

Look at all my foolish attempts at being someone of importance.
Sometimes I manage to look in at my life from the outside.
Alas, I just always end up pitying myself.

And you know what's funny?
I expect myself not to pity me, yet, I'm purposely destroying
myself via pills, blades, and sick emotions.
I don't want to die or anything like that.
I just take the pills, seeing how many I can take until I go
comatose.
I press the blade to my skin, seeing how much blood I can spill.
I feel all these things, seeing how much damage I can do to
things and people.
And you.

Destruction is my life now. But it's furtive destruction.
Is that really any better?

Tell me...do you pity me, too?
I thought so.
No hard feelings, though.
It's expected.

Give me hope again; make this sick feeling in my stomach cease.
It's been almost a year since I've believed in the beautiful things
that life allegedly has to offer me.
It's just been so long.
It bothers me.
But not really.

Because I'm comfortably numb and happily apathetic.
I just...don't try anymore.

I foresee that my pessimism will eventually be the end of me.

The line which divides my dreams and reality is beginning to blur.

Or fade out of existence.
I ignore the banalities of both, often finding myself lost in my thoughts.

I've felt a bit more lonely these past few days.
Except lonely in a less conventional way.

People have the ability to control their lives, and most of what it contains of.
If that's so, then do I really choose pain over pleasure every single time?
Maybe.
Maybe it's the way pain makes my thoughts race that makes it appealing.
Or maybe it's just the amusement of my naive struggling that makes it more appealing than pleasure.
Or maybe it's the seldom times that I feel pleasure rather than pain that makes me appreciative of the pleasure.

What an enigma.
Referring to...?
That's an enigma in itself.

An Infinite, Disconsolate Perpetuity

Sitting here in the lovely world of
Illusions caused by anti-depressants, anti-psychotics, and anti-everything else.
I'm ready to be numb again.
Oh medication, please save me from myself.
Even though I know you won't.
Wishful thinking has never hurt anyone though, right?
Or at least nowhere near as much as people hurt themselves.

As I've stated before (or perhaps simply thought), nothing is as useless nor as beneficial as extensive thought. Ultimately, these enigmatic thoughts will have no meaning; they only set me apart from the majority right now, for I am in a constant state of solitude due to my cognizance. Though this is somewhat of an ailment, I am still infinitely grateful for it. Even if it does mean I'm alone most of the time.

They (who?) say that the fear of death is a characteristic of all living things.
I'm not afraid to die...

What does that make me?

Nestor Ramirez

To be completely honest, I don't know why my writing is in this book, since the majority of it isn't even poetry. Most of my work is just a collection of thoughts that I put down on paper. If anything, I find my writing to be conversational instead of poetic or instructional. I want my writing to be more than just something the readers will pass over, I want it to be a conversation; I want the reader to form their own opinions and argue against it, or agree with it, or tell me why they think it's the dumbest piece of writing they've seen in their whole lives- as long as they do more than just read.

    As a side note, I apologize for any grammatical errors in advance, in case they do exist. I have a strict policy of not having a policy for proof-reading and editing my work. I'm just not that kind of guy. If my readers overanalyze and think it's an example of hubris, so be it, but I don't find it so- I just don't enjoy proofreading my work. Sorry.

"There comes a time when silence is betrayal." In the presence of extraordinary prejudice, those who advocate equality must stand with those that have been affected. Sadly, the world rarely does this. People stand out and protest when their natural rights have been trampled on, however when the same happens to others, they share an appalling silence.

When the rights of others have been degraded, it doesn't matter whether or not we are affected. Instead we should perpetuate justice for all of mankind, regardless of the demographic in question. Catholic authorities say nothing when Anti-Semitic messages resonate throughout the community, but "Happy Holidays" is worthy of waging a war over. Americans speak out when someone on a radio show yells obscenities, but we are silent when the citizens Myanmar are killed by their own military for simply pleading for equal rights. Is that not what we suffered and endured for decades? Centuries? What makes us worthy of global compassion, yet makes the Sudanese unworthy of anything - save for a cold shoulder?

If we are to advocate equal rights, we must hold all people to an equal standard. Not only does or silence betray our fellow man, it betrays our morals and philosophies. Instead of wallowing in hypocrisy, we should rise up and speak in a synchronized voice for our human rights – not just for ourselves, but also for the less fortunate.

"Judge not lest ye be Judged"

Words present in everyone's philosophy
But what is life philosophy
Besides a blatant hypocrisy
Because in everyone's eyes
Judging others is wrong
Unless they're different,
or even worse
if you judge them
They teach us that the Bible is the good book
As if all the others are bad ones.
And I'm forced to sit up here and apologize.
"Sorry, religion ain't my cup of tea
I prefer literature
Books like 'The Metamorphosis'
Where a great flood leaves
Only two humans,
The two pious ones
Yet their names are not Noah."
I'm forced to apologize.
"Sorry, I'm in a religious minority.
But that doesn't mean the minority is wrong.
We're all wrong.
The way we treat each other is wrong."
I'll apologize one more time,
The last time.
"Sorry, I'm not the same.
Sorry, I won't conform,
But I'm open to suggestions."
But I'm not the only one who should apologize.
Everyone needs to apologize
Because the good book, excuse me, A good book
Says, "Judge not, lest ye be judged."
Realize your mistakes and tell everyone you're sorry
Tell them you love your neighbor,
Regardless of what books they read.
Because equality is never wrong
Regardless of what religion you preach.

I believe in optimism.

It's only natural that individuals, particularly those treading the turbulent and treacherous teenage years, develop a sense of disillusionment along the road to cognitive maturation- some more so than others. I, for example, developed a cynic disposition towards my classmates, and society as a whole, after enduring the tortures of elementary and middle school, which ranged from bullying, ridicule, harassment and everything existent in the spectrum of physical and emotional abuse. To put it simply, I didn't expect anyone to befriend me, and frankly, I didn't care who liked me or not. How I portrayed myself in public was of no concern to others as far as I knew. I was a loner- an apathetic and depressed child. However, regardless of my solidarity or emotional distress, there was always that small light in the depths of my mind that told me one day, things will get better. Within the abysmal melancholy that existed in me, there was a candle that brought light into that darkness, and ultimately put a smile back in my face. I firmly believe that this optimism that existed deep within me caused me to break out my hollow existence and brought substance to my being.

Optimism has been a prominent aspect in my personality ever since those days. In fact, I was right deep down; my situation did improve, my emotional stability strengthened, and I'm happier than ever. I have friends who support me, a stable job, an amicable disposition, and the most important luxury of all: life. When I turn on my T.V. and see the names of those who've made the ultimate sacrifice miles away from home, I pay my respects to them and think to myself, "well, at least we won't have the same plenipotentiary man as our leader in a year from now." After looking at the houses in my neighborhood after Hurricane Wilma tore them apart, I didn't frown. Instead, I told myself that there was work to be done in order to rejuvenate these destroyed communities.

I've come to learn that hard-ships are just one of the many ephemeron present in our long lives, and that one should never "sweat the small stuff." An optimistic demeanor can become a self-fulfilling prophecy; just by thinking things will get better, in reality they just might. As evident throughout history, man always overcomes the problems they face. They always rebuild in order to continue living. Therefore, I know I should always hold my head up high, and work towards a better tomorrow. In the famous words of Sam Cooke, "It's been a long time comin', but I know a change gon' come."

I Never

I never told you this, but
The smell of vanilla entices me,
and injects my mind with so many memories
of us, two flowers in a field of weeds.
I never told you this, but
Green jackets are my favorite.
I walk through a frigid ether,
warmed only by the thoughts of your grip
on this thin fabric.
I never told you this, but
Emerson is more than an author.
He is a gateway into our minds
and a foundation for our perspectives,
until I told you:
"I hate quotations, tell me what you know."
I never told you this, but
Your glance turns me to stone.
You're an enchantress with hair of silk,
yet I stand here petrified.
Life will only return
when you smile.
I never told you this, but
I can never tell you this enough.
Te amo.

Ode to the Weekdays

The Holy day, the day of worship
is, for You, a day to renew the foundation-
you should prepare for the following week.
The week will bring disturbances,
hindrances, and inquiries that will
challenge your philosophies,
so You will approach these questions with
quotations and verses, followed by a smirk that says
"I am right and you are wrong."
You will look down on those who tread a different trail
from that high pedestal of morality and tell them
"your views of life are myopic,
can't you see that you are not right?
that life is not what you think it is?
that your life isn't yours?
that this is how you should live?"
You judge others and tell them they're wrong
-even when the majority of the world says otherwise-
But it's ok, this book makes you infallible.
Even though the weekdays are truly harmless,
You view them as zealots of evil, or even more ironically,
heretics.
so when Sunday comes, all Your judgments,
hypocritical actions, condescending words,
will all be erased, because you acted
in the name of God.

I recently watched the electoral debates that, at this point, are being held every other day, and I've noticed that the candidates running for president of the United States have a certain elegance to their speeches and monologues; they speak with perfect poise and tone after every question is asked. So much so, that they're monotonous and robotic. The participants regurgitate pre-recorded words, phrases, and statements they learned only minutes before in order to convince us that this pseudo-intellectual campaign is real and meaningful. This is American politics at its core- or, at the very least, the basis of its presentation.

After careful analysis of American politics and partisan relations (and by careful analysis, I mean completely biased against both parties), I have stumbled across three fundamental truths. These three truths serve as a direct correlation between American politics and Life itself, giving me a deeper understanding of the world that surrounds me on a daily basis.

Life is a war, and those that refuse to destroy the enemy will fall through the cracks of mediocrity.

Sun Tzu's "The Art Of War" is a piece of literature which has become iconic, primarily as a result of the similarities his strategies share with daily life. However in reality, life is much more subtle than this. It is a war of attrition, and in order to rise above the average, you must destroy, kill, betray and fight without your spectators knowing of this. You must be a congressman; comfort those around you to gain their trust, yet follow your own hidden agendas. You must be a president; tell the people that under your rule, the war(s) will end, the economy will be stimulated and life will be grand, but simultaneously plot terrorist attacks and private alliances when the cameras are off.

If one doesn't become corrupted and aggressive, one will never rise above the average- the "middle class". It is well known that "good guys finish last," and from what the news actively shows me every day, the American public only remember the murderers, the rapists, the "headlines," and completely forget about the philanthropists, the social activists and the romantics. The latter will never ascend past the title of "good guy"- a title which doesn't provide food for their family. The former will be known for all of history, gaining fame and fortune through press conferences, book sales and interviews. Therefore, the only way to succeed in life is to go against oneself and ones morals. Relinquish your beliefs and succumb to the temptation of infamy, because only this will grant you access to the upper echelons of society.

All men are created equal, but some are more equal than others.

Equality is a word that has been thrown around haphazardly over the recent decades. Everyone wants equal rights, and all it takes is the whip of a pen to create new legislature. However, this is not enough. We have become satisfied with simple laws and statements that say "You are an equal," and don't bother to realize just how unequal everyone is treated in America.

Politicians use this to their advantage. They stand at the podium and speak on the rights minorities will be granted under their guidance, and we are won over immediately. Do we not realize that even under such laws, everyone will be viewed through myopic eyes by those in power? The judicial system continues to use racial profiling and socioeconomic statistics to predict which areas will be ridden with crime, instead of providing new systems to end these violent trends. The government still consists primarily of rich, white, catholic men who have nothing better to do than see their wallets grow thicker from lobbyists and oil trades, instead of focusing on the plagues ruining the streets of my country. We are not equals. We are not on the same level as the politicians, as they continue to show us everyday. We are only worthy of rushed legislature that says "don't make fun of these people," instead of laws that state "this is what we will do to stimulate growth of bad communities." Remember this: when politicians- and even just ordinary people- tell you that "you are an equal," they only say it so their malicious endeavors are overlooked.

Love is a mob mentality.

There are many loved politicians and presidents that retain such a status for many years. John F. Kennedy, Bobby Kennedy and Franklin D. Roosevelt are examples of this. The majority of Americans will state these names when asked "which politician do you like best?" However, if one asks why they feel this way, many will be left speechless. Why do they feel this way indeed? To most, there is no reason other than the fact that their response has been reiterated so often by others around them.

In our generation, love is the same way. People don't fall in love anymore, they dive into it without realizing how deep the waters are. There is no true "love" anymore- only the demand for acceptance remains. We see others entering relationships and hunger for our own, so instead of looking for their "ideal pair," they grab whatever they can get. This is the effects of a mob mentality; we try to follow in the footsteps of others in order to gain acceptance in our community. This creates a false expectation about love that becomes deep rooted in our psyche. We see it only as something that helps us gain popularity and status in the inner circle of friends. Politicians gain votes in the same fashion. Many of those who vote in the primary elections don't know anything about the platform of their favorite candidate. All they know is that "all my friends are totally voting for them, so that means they must be good." We must fight against this mob mentality and discover the true meaning behind "love." It isn't just a status symbol, it is what drives us to go against the norm and express our latent emotions.

These truths shed light on this world which I've found so trivial and quixotic up until this moment. I feel as if the politicians know these truths themselves, and utilize them to their advantage, to grab the nation in a stranglehold and choke the life out of the oblivious majority.

I wish I could become President one day, but I don't know if I'm *that* indifferent.

Timothy Reavis

A Stroll in the Fall

So they floated hand in hand
Under the gentle sky
And past the grand hollow
That bleeds, because the Fall
Has seized the land – and killed it red,
And warns against their clasp's might.

They might
Plunge the wood – but relenting is his hand
For his heart burns red
To gaze at the lovely sky.
But falling for the Fall,
They plunge the wood, and depart from the sky and the hollow.

A heart on here altar, his chest now hollow,
They wonder in their clasp's might,
While the foliage dances about them in the Fall.
But no mind is paid – for the world is her hand,
Her blue eyes – his sky
And her hair – his autumn red.

Over their heads, the oaks loom yellow, orange, now red –
As they skip further away from the hollow.
The path winds like a serpent, and eats the sky,
As the Fall performs its blinding might –
And tickles his brow with the branches, approves their hand,
As they continue to indulge in the Fall.

So deeper into the hanging Fall
The wood has grown a fiery red.
Weary, they turn about, hand in hand,
Desiring to rest under the hollow.
But the ironclad oaks, established in finality's might
Deny them return to the visible sky.

Where, where is the visible sky?
No, he has bitten the apple of her eye, and the Fall
Has seized the land – and clenched them in its might.
At every turn, the wood burns red,
And denies them rest, under the hollow –
As Hawthorne ponders their hand.

Gone is the sky, eternal is the autumn red.
And like a stone in the fall, is the hollow might of their hand.

Dissection of *A Stroll in the Fall*

The obvious symbolism purpose of the poem is to mirror the initial downfall of Adam and Eve, and to perpetuate the notion that it was their idolatrous love for one another that initiated the Fall. This is accomplished in the dual symbolism of the ending words, and the metaphors used throughout the poem to allude to Adam and Eve. The word "Fall" serves as the most obvious emblem of the poem, the two meanings of the word (as in the fall season and the Fall of Man) are virtually interchangeable throughout the poem. The Fall serves as the primary setting of the story in both senses, and is the controlling element of the poem's purpose. The "sky" in the poem serves the place of the omnipotent and loving Father, which in the beginning shares a loving relationship with the man until the woman leads him into the forest, which is ablaze with the "Fall" foliage. The hollow in the story is a symbol of Jesus Christ, the embodiment of the invisible and intangible God, which can be paralleled to the tangible quality of a tree as to the intangible quality of the sky, though they are both part of nature. The hollow is assumed to take the role of Jesus in when first mentioned in the first stanza, when the hollow "bleeds" (line 4), because "the Fall has seized the land – and killed it red□" (line4-5). Jesus was made to bleed as an ultimate result of the Fall, as the hollow "bleeds" (or turns red) as a result of the season of fall. The color red serves multiple purposes in the story – it is associated with blood, the Fall season, and fire through many places in the poem. This is to give the poem and intense feel and tone, red being associated with the Fall – which is the physical setting – and fire, being the result of the Fall.

This poem's intention is to take the reader along with this couple's journey from graceful love to being lost in the fall as a result of the woman's insistence that they enter the wood. The poem begins with the couple in the open, "under the gentle sky," in a rapturous love for one another and the enjoyment of the sky. The usage of the word "float" conveys this point, the two being in love with one another while "floating" as the sky floats. The Fall has "seized the land" in the first stanza, being symbolic of the fall season and the Fall of man. In the second stanza the woman desires to enter the wood, lit up with fall foliage (a mechanism of the symbolic Fall) while the man is somewhat reluctant. This is relative to the original story of Adam and Eve, because Eve was the first to take the bite of the apple, and then seduced Adam into doing the same. His heart desires to "gaze at the sky," but he "falls for the Fall," meaning he was enticed by the colors of the fall wood. They then "plunge" the wood (which is relative to the manner of plunging into a dive or literal fall) and depart from the wood (which is symbolic of the departure of Man from God). His idolatrous love for her is then made evident in the first line of the third stanza, having chose to disobey the hollow and enter the wood, and putting her above God in a figurative sense. This image is accomplished in the use of the phrase "her altar," in which he lays his heart, which is an image typically associated with worship. They then "wonder" about the wood (which is what Adam and Eve must have done having been expelled from the Garden) as the "Fall" foliage dances about them, which is figurative for them being in the middle of the Fall. Initially, he pays no mind to the fall (or Fall) because he is enraptured by his love, evident in the last three lines of the third stanza. But as the poem continues, she begins to assimilate into the fall, conveying the sense that she is his fall. The fourth stanza serves to present the image of the couple plunging deeper into the fall, as the colors grow more intense, eventually becoming red, just as her hair is red. This is to tie the image of red to her hair and to the fall together, and as to incorporate them both as his Fall (or fall). The metaphor in line 21 alludes directly to the serpent – the path "winds like a serpent" in order to convey the disobedience of their journey, and also to explain that they are going further into the forest (or the fall). The serpent then "eats the sky" – this means that they have plunged deep enough into the wear there is no longest any visible sky, and also to insinuate that the serpent has led them away form God, or the sky. The next few lines' purpose (line 23-24) is to make evident the approval of the fall upon their relationship.

The fifth stanza bears the twist in the plot. The wood has grown a "fiery red," and they have grown weary of the fall. They desire to return to the hollow and the sky, but cannot escape the forest and find their way out. The use of word "ironclad" serves to establish the oaks as immovable and permanent, foreshadowing their permanence within the fall. The sixth stanza has grown frantic, and voices the couple's cry for the sky. The next metaphor gives a direct answer as to why they cannot exit the wood. He has bitten the apple of her eye" – he is the apple of her eye (which hints at her idolatrous love for him) while in turn he has smitten himself in "biting the apple" and following her in the first place; so he has bitten and destroyed himself. The forest burning red is symbolic of the hell they have now found themselves in as a result of the fall. The reference to Hawthorne may seem out of place, but if one knows Hawthorne than this is a relative association. Hawthorne believed that the Original Sin was Adam and Eve's idolatrous love for one another, and thus describes the love that the couple has for one another in the poem (proof for this assertion is ready upon request).

The envoy serves to solidify their position in the fall. The sky is gone, and the burning red of the fall is eternal. The last simile embodies perfectly their relationship. Like a "stone in the Fall" has a dual meaning. The union of their hand has become so intertwined that they can no longer detach from one another, and become as solid as stone (evident in the intentional use of "their hand," the couple now seeming to have only one joined hand). This fused relationship is "like a stone in the fall" in the literal sense that stones are cold in the fall, because the fall temperature is cold, just as their relationship has proven to be cold and disdainful as holding a stone in the fall. The union of their hand also serves as a weight in a suspended fall, which the two cannot escape because their hands have become one as a symbol of their idolatrous dependence of one another as opposed to dependence on God. This can also be seen as an allusion to "Sinners in the Hands of an Angry God," when John Edwards compares the inability of sinners escaping the fall into hell to a stone falling through a spider web. Thus the couple is stuck in the fall as a result of their relationship.

Apathy

A dead leaf falls from
The branch that sustains and lives –
And never returns.

Dissection of *Apathy*

This is a highly symbolic poem which contains a central Biblical reference that must be known to understand the poem fully. The allusion is to the book of John, chapter 15, verses 1-4; in this passage, Jesus says that "[He] is the true vine, and my Father is the Gardner. He cuts off every branch in me that bears no fruit, while every branch that does bear fruit he prunes so that it will be even more fruitful□ No branch can bear fruit by itself; it must remain in the vine. Neither can you bear fruit unless you remain in me."

The dead leaf is the modern Christian. The follower of Christ is to be an extension of Christ Himself, and "bear fruit" (which is a reference to the fruits of the Spirit described in 1 Corinthians, which include love, joy, faith, mercy, forgiveness, etc.) which resembles that of Christ Himself. The dead leaf is the modern Christian in the sense that for the most part, no fruit has been brought forth. The fruits of the Spirit are the result of being "saturated in the Spirit," or remaining in Christ. To remain in Christ is to walk in the Spirit, and to be truly alive. The church is a pile of dry leaves because we have not remained "in Christ" in the literal and actual sense. The church, or "Christian," may claim to be in the sentimental sense, but in reality, he may have never truly experienced God's love and power in a real way. This is due to the fact that our faith has become bland and ceremonially based, to the point of being deathly boring and lacking any real connection to God Himself. And because the believer has never truly experienced God, and never spend time in His presence, the Christian falls away from god (or what he perceives as being God, being "church stuff," which is not really God). The last line is the observation of these occurrences, and the rate at which the person usually returns to this life is as rare as a dead leaf returning to its place in the tree. The tree, or branch (symbolic of God) is in the church, but the person's inability to return to the tree is due to the perception of bland church life being God, not to the true God life being bland.

Later

Man has not evolved, but accumulated,
And weighs the earth off its course.
What will happen, when frustrated,
The earth shakes, in prevailing force?
God said this would happen - our heavy hearts
Would weigh us down, with the earth.
And so as the sea He parts,
So shall we also be, severed from the planet's girth.
Man has piled his empires, like trophies of rust
That collect dust, and don't impress the sun.
Stockpile guns, missiles, nukes, just
In case God spoils our fun.
Child, run – run to the hill,
The stage is set, and death is our thrill.

Dissection of *Later*

The purpose of this poem is to reveal the impending disaster that humans will inevitably face. But not only does it hint at the coming danger, but it also seeks to assert that God has set in place a time of intervention. Line 1 alludes to the current assumption that the planet is becoming overwhelmed by the human population, and is being drained rapidly of its sources and ability to sustain. The earth "shakes, in prevailing force" because it desires to liberate itself from our leeching society, which God has set in place for the future. This is made evident in line 5, alluding to when Jesus said "If those days had not been cut short, no one would survive, but for the sake of the elect those days will be shortened." So God will cut our days short here on earth at the second coming of Jesus, and "[severe] us from the planet's girth." The allusion to the parting of the sea in line 7 supports the image of the severing of man from the earth, much as the sea was divided into two halves for the Jews in the Old Testament. This also adds another dimension to the poem, giving the image of man as a whole being divided from the earth, but being divided into the faithful and wicked, as in two precise halves. In the third quatrain, the poem is brought to the current time and mindset, man having "piled empires" for himself. The simile "like trophies of rust" asserts to novelty nature of our kingdoms when viewed objectively from the viewpoint of the greater universe. This greater view is conveyed in the next line, with the sun being unimpressed by man's empires. The next line delves further into man's current mindset of war and self-guardedness. The last line of the third quatrain reveals man's motive for his self-guardedness, man hoping to somehow counter God with masses of weapons upon the time of intervention (which is predicted to happen by the Bible). Man's desires to counter God so they can continue in their "fun" sin and their own ways without having to worry about moral obligation to God. The couplet's first line is a Biblical allusion as well. The Bible says that times will be so drastic and horrifying in the end of days that the people will run into the valleys and cry out to the rocks to fall on them. The advice given to the child is counter to this action, advising the child to run to the top of the hill instead of the valley, so that the rocks may not fall on him, so that the child may remain apart from the desperate and possibly insane whole of humanity and remain safe on the mountain. Another verse in the Bible also says, "Who may ascend the hill of the Lord? He who has clean hands and a pure heart." So the line of advice is also a call to morality in the current time of hideous immorality; so the line of advice serves a current purpose for the child and a purpose for the future. The last line alludes to the notion that all the precursors to the "end of days" (or time of God's intervention) is near; that the "stage is set." The Bible also talks about an odd phenomena that will occur in the end of days, in which man will suffer from a plague so gruesome that they will desire death, but "death will not find them." This is what is meant in the last phrase, "death is our thrill," in the sense that men will desire death. This can also allude to the massive war that will break out during that time, in which men will take pleasure in killing each other. When looked upon in all its allusion, this poem is quite bothering and disdainful, yet offers an interesting insight into what "Later" will be like for man.

Epigrams

Restraint
Time is in our minds and mines.

Empty
Threats don't move,
Until the world's on fire.

Joseph Shambley

Have you Seen the World Today?

Have you seen the world today?
There are dealers selling pot
A few feet from the very spot
That your sons and daughters work on their jump shot

Have you seen the world today?
On every street you see gang bangers
Walking around so called "twisting up their fangers"
A world where the wrong color is potential danger

Have you seen the world today?
Our government justifies
Losing a few good lives
To make our oil prices rise

Have you seen the world today?
Countries going to war over religion
It doesn't matter whether you're Muslim or Christian
People are allowed to make their own decision

Have you seen the world today?
One thing most people don't see
There are people starving on the streets
While most of us waste more than we can eat

I have seen the world today
Honestly I don't like it
Maybe one day we can be united
And stand up and fight it

What's Your Purpose?

They say we were put here for a purpose
Whether it is to be a preacher giving a church service
Being a thug who snatches women's purses
Or even being a rapper who lives his life through verses

Some of us don't know our soul purpose
Even after we have been on a thousand searches
After awhile we may get a little discouraged
Until you finally succeed in your searching

Once you have found your life's purpose
Be sure that you always nourish it
So that one day it will flourish
Because to some what never occurs is
How we are forever cursed with
Not knowing how close to the end Earth is.

Aaron Simrell

Why do I write dark poetry? I'm sure many wondered this. Though to be honest it's not something I could answer easily. To better understand how and why I write then you must understand my intentions. I moved quite a lot throughout my life, my mother died in a car crash which I was in. I never really saw my father until her death which makes about ten years. I then lived with the typical step mom cliché. Though all these things never really brought me to write so dark. I love heavy metal, horror films and hate most people. I read tarot cards practice Wicca and love violent video games but then again it wasn't my reason for writing. I guess its a lot deeper then that. Not cause and effect but a sort of destiny. I was just drawn to dark poetry and other writing such as that. Though in my eyes it's no where near that of darkness. To me it's more like the light. For that's what it brings out. You can not value the light if you've never been in the dark. You can not realize what is good without knowing full well what is bad. I write not so much as to express myself as it is to open other people's eyes and to entertain. People see me and assume so many things. They assume a bad child hood, poor grades and a bad attitude. That may be a fraction of the truth for I did have a bad child hood. Though for those who are willing to know me they see what I really am, a great and loyal friend, a soul mate that will never stop loving to a very special person, a smart guy with a very positive outlook on life. Not the religion fanatic positive but a way of seeing life for what it is. It sucks! just flat out sucks and can not seem worth it. Though on other occasions it's as perfect as heaven on earth. This will never change and continue to go back and forth. though most times more negative then positive. Moving so much as a child and seeing so many things has taught me this well. For example is my mother's death. She died in a car crash when I was thirteen. I then moved to live with my dad and a you know what step mom. Most others would find this bad and just want to give up. Though to me I knew better things would come along. This came true as I met the girl I fell in love with. She became the center of my universe and my future wife. Now if my mother never passed away I would have never moved and met this girl. Negative and positive will always exist. As the age old question goes, "You see a glass half of water on a table. Is it half full or half empty?" Some say empty and others say full. Though my first thought when asked this question was a bit odd. I simply thought if I was thirsty or not. Such a simple thought at first but when applied to life it can mean so much more. Stop thinking of life as positive or negative, good or bad, unlivable or livable. Just take life as it is and don't look so deep into meaningless things. Instead look deeper into those things that matter. Take a second look at that Goth kid walking down the street. Don't just assume what you think is obvious. Don't let others set the standard of what you should think. Dream to think and think to dream. When you can understand that then you can enjoy life in all situations. This is why I write the way I do. So wake up, open your eyes and SEE!

Now and Forever

You ease my mind in every way
You ease my soul every day
You ease my heart making it grow with affection
You ease my life making it seem like perfection
You ease my thoughts just by your presence
You ease my dreams just by your essence
I love you, I love you, I love you now and forever
You make me hope were together for many, many years
You make me cry just by seeing your tears
You make me happy with just a kiss
You make me sad when its you that I miss
You make me depressed when I can't hear your voice
You make me choose you, you are my final choice
I love you, I love you, I love you now and forever
You are the girl I love and want to wed
You are the only girl ill ever share a bed
You are the girl I will someday call my wife
You are the only girl for me only one in my life
You are the only girl I will ever call my lover
You are the only girl I will be happy to make a mother
I love you, I love you, I love you now and forever
You love me when I do something bad
You love me even when you're mad
You love me so much I can't explain
You love me so much I'll never complain
You love me with all your heart
You love me so much I know we'll never be apart
I love you...I love you...I love you now and forever

You Don't Belong

Slit your wrists and hope you die
Do this every night and cry
Always the same thing the same tone
Laying there just wishing you weren't alone
This is what you think there in bed
Just laying there wishing you were dead
See the blood trickle down your wrist
Think of killing everyone on your hit list
Is this how you want to live your life
Not living at all balanced at the tip of a knife
Pretending your happy so others don't ask
Going through life wearing this mask
It's so sad you say you wish for nothing
Even though all you ever want is something
Cast away your pain cast away you hate
Shatter your mask before it's too late
Throw away that blade and let those scars heal
Open your heart and allow yourself to feel
Leave the darkness and step into the light
Don't hold back everything will be alright
This is your world and you belong
Live your life and don't let anyone say you're wrong

Angel

Your beauty is like a virus
That infects my heart and mind
With each passing day it grows and grows
Until it drives me crazy
Crazy for you, but you don't stop there,
For when you wrap your arms around me
It feels as if a heavenly blanket protects
Me from this dark and lonely world
Your voice is like a soft whisper that
Echoes in my mind and speeds up my heartbeat
For it seems like a sin to hear the
Voice of an angel as beautiful as you
Even now as I think of about you
A warm feeling spreads through my body
For I feel as if I could love for an eternity
You make me feel that everything that has happened in my life
Has lead up to this point in time, this time with you.
For you make me feel complete,
Whole, and at peace because all I want is you
And I'd stop time just to keep it that way, for I love you
I love you with all my heart and
I can only hope you feel the same

Crack Samurai

I come bursting out of the shadows like a Samurai on crack
swinging and chopping till I leave a bunch of bodies in one big
stack
I'll slit your throat and stab you through the heart
you try to run and hide but I'm just too damn smart
I find you and torture you in more than one way
till you learn your better off if you just stay
I love it when you try to stand your ground and fight back
but most the time I'll take you down with just one smack
I suddenly attack you with the speed of a viper
then I throw my ninja star with the accuracy of a sniper
I hit your friend a mile away in the forehead
before you know what going on you both drop dead
I walk off into the shadows with your money back into my shack
leaving you dead and gone waiting for the next time to attack

Creatures of the Night

They hide in the shadows just out of your sight
Operating in silence for they're the creatures of the night
They fly through the air without the slightest detection
Showing no mercy and living life without affection
They survive by sucking the blood from
your body and life from your soul
When they finish with their feeding you're
under they're complete control
They are no longer of the living and yet not quiet dead
Infecting our world with each passing night as they spread
They control us all from behind a shroud of darkness
Ruling us like lambs for the slaughter for they're cold and
heartless
They know they can wipe us out in one night and we can't resist
So I suggest to you all that you just be happy you still exist

Darkness

grief, sorrow, hatred they spread through me like a fire
twisted, distorted, uncontrollable is my life as it becomes dire
cold, dark, hard is my heart as I just try to exist
kill, steal, hurt are the dark thoughts I try to resist
I live my life with these thoughts and feelings
rejecting them all no matter just how appealing
I try and open my heart to those who care
even though this world is cruel and love is very rare
I do this all so when I die suddenly one night
people know that however dark this world I always put up a fight

Desire

Your life is nothing but a grain of sand, a grain of sand in this vast dessert we call existence. You sit there waiting and waiting for your purpose that makes you different from so many others but you wait for something that will never come. For your only purpose is to live. Live to create more life. It is the only purpose of every living thing, to live and create more life like a meaningless virus that spreads through time only to survive because of desire. The desire for more the desire for what we do not already have and until you realize and let go of these desires you will always be nothing but a grain of sand.

Emptiness

I look at her picture trying to remember her, that feeling that I once knew. As I stare at her face I feel as if I've become inhuman, become something with no heart or soul, for I feel no grief, no sorrow, no hatred and no joy, just emptiness. as if everything in me just died and rotted till there was no sign of it left, but try as I must nothing happens, so I stare harder and harder just wishing for some feeling of joy or sorrow so I know my time with her was not just some twisted dream. So I sit here waiting for the person that can awaken the feeling I once knew and fill the emptiness I now know.

I Remember

I still remember those feelings
I had for you oh so very long ago
They are etched in my memory
For me to ever know
I still remember the first day I
Was so lucky as to lay eyes upon you
You where the cutest girl there even
Though you wouldn't think its true
I still remember the first time we
Spoke and how nervous I became
I had such a hard time talking to
You I couldn't even say your first name
I still remember how you smiled every
Time you would look at me
I couldn't help but smile back as
I was falling in love with every guarantee
I still remember the very first
Time I called asking you out
You had me worried but then
Answered yes without a doubt
I still remember our first official
Date where we had our first kiss
The day was so perfect it was total
Bliss and the only place I would like to exist
I still remember the night I asked
You to be by my side forever in life
You became the women that would
Make me happy by being my wife
I still remember how I fell in love
With you month by month week by week and every day
I still remember this because my
Love for you is forever growing and forever here to stay

Life

You were there for me in my darkest hour
Making me burst with love realizing its absolute power
You broke down the wall I built around my heart
Showing me the light realizing we couldn't be apart
You mad me laugh whenever I was sad
Made me cry whenever I was mad
You made me express my true emotions welled up inside
Rather that keeping them in because of foolish pride
You made me see life for what it really is, you
For there is no life without you and you better believe it's true
You are the one I'll marry and proudly call my wife
For all I can think about is you and me for the rest of our life

Love

This feeling I do not know how to describe, it is just there
There like the moon and the stars at night
There like a single rose in a never ending field of darkness
This feeling is like a heavenly light cutting through the sorrows
Of my soul till it pierces my heart
This feeling can never die for it can only be put to sleep
Waiting to be awakened from its slumber
And you my angel riding upon your chariot of light
Have awaken this feeling and named it love
Love me like that
love me as long as your heart still beats
love me till the grim reaper reaps
love me till I'm dead and gone
love me and I can do no wrong
love till time comes to an end
love and all wounds will mend
love me as long as were together
love me and ill be yours forever

MENTAL^LY UNSOUND

I am your worst nightmare come to life
stalking through the shadows holding my knife
I am silent and deadly like death nipping at your feet
if you try and fight me you will certainly face defeat
I am completely insane and mentally unsound
death and chaos follow me all around
I am the one that sneaks in your room at night
killing you dead and cold without even a fight
I am unstoppable, inconsolable, and ready to kill
don't try to run, nobody matches my skill

Moonlit Lake

I go there everyday leaving behind
all my troubles and worries
Going there to escape reality and
live my favorite stories
I can do what I want, go where I
please without even the slightest care
It's my paradise from the real world
That is cruel and never fair
I think of those who have a special place in my heart
Thinking most of one special person I can't stand to be apart
I think of us cuddled together on a beautiful winter night
Just holding each other thinking of the future with no end in
sight
I just lay there with you forever forgetting the anxiety of my day
Holding you tight and looking at the
stars with only the slightest thing to say
I kiss you gently on the lips while stoking your beautiful hair
Then I whisper sweet nothings in your ear through the cold night
air
I can think of no other place I'd rather
be than here with you next to the moonlit lake
But as I think of this I come back
To reality remembering its all fake
I now sit in my room with reality making me want to scream
Thinking of nothing but you and how I wish it wasn't a dream

My Lost Hero

She disappeared from my world in just one night
leaving me in desperation sorrow and fright
she was my world everything I wish I could be
never thought shed die right in front of me were I can see
she seemed so indestructible always being so strong
when she laid there unconscious it all seemed so wrong
she just laid in the street making no noise just being there
all I could do is just stand there and stare
she was always there being my hero
but now her time is gone, ticked down to zero
she still gives me strength keeping me strong
giving me advice on life either right or wrong
she is forever on my mind and in my heart
so I know no matter how far away, we're never apart

Paradise

Roses are red and violets are blue,
But this means nothing compared to you
For you are my morning and my night
For you are the one who has awakened
Me from my eternal slumber
For you are the one who reached down from the heavens
And guided me to paradise and that
Paradise is where I plan to stay
Stay with you in the heavens above
Like a god and goddess of love
That is what we shall be, for you have
Stolen my heart like no other
And locked it away, but do not worry
My heart is your and that is where it shall stay

Scar

I sit here looking at my scar, the scar that ended my life, the scar that tore me from the inside out, and the very scar that taught there truly is no god. I hat this scar but I can't imagine my life without it. It sits there like I little reminder that there is no reason to this madness this chaos we call life for it is short and pointless. I sit here looking at my scar wishing it was her and not me that had a second chance for when she died all that I knew, all that I loved, and all that I believed just died and withered away leaving but hatred, grief, and sorrow. Now I sit here cursing this wretched scar for it has left me with no need for life yet no desire for death

Soul Mate

Sense her presence and all your worries are gone
Feel her touch and nothing seems wrong
Hear her voice and watch it tame the beast inside
Look into her eyes and realize there is nothing you need to hide
Hug her tightly and see all the love she has to give
Kiss her lips and think she's the only reason you live
Watch your souls unite and entwine slowly becoming one
Realize when you're with her, your life, has just begun

Time

God, many worship this idea, this idea of a supreme being of the universe who created us all and the world we live in, but god is just that an idea an illusion created so many years ago by a civilization long since dead. For they were captives of the only thing that can truly be called god and that is time. For time is what created us all time is what made this world this, very existence. for time is what made us try harder, push farther and hope our end will never come, even though nothing escapes the vastness of time. For it alone decides when you are finished.

Everything Will Be Alright

Shh, it's starting again that thing that haunts your nightmares
It's so unfair to you and it feels like nobody cares
I know you're trying to ignore it, thinking it doesn't exist
I know you'll get that knot in your throat you can never resist
Shh, be strong, be brave, everything will be alright
To you this is hell and you end up there all of the time
I know your thoughts begin to race and you ask yourself "Why?"
I know your walls begin to crumble and now you begin to cry
Shh, its ok let me hold you close and wipe away that tear
I've come to make you feel better so you have nothing left to fear
I know the noise is loud and scary right outside your door
I know your heart stops every time something hits the floor
Shh, I'm here now, don't listen to that noise and just hold me tight
I'll hold you against my chest and I promise everything will be alright
I know I make you feel safe and that's just what I do
I know as long as you need me I'll always be here just for you

Ties of Fate

She drifts away without a worry of mind
I feel our ties of fate reach their limit
I watch her become not something of mine
Is this our fate? Our destiny? Is it?
I know she'll be gone from my odd world
Casting me further into the darkness
My lasting heart becomes dark, hard and cold
This is it, the end, my growing weakness
This can not be. Should I not be worried?
Should I not fear the loss of a loved one?
Do I not want this? The joy is carried
Have I lost the battle? Have I not won?!
This is my fate, the end, my feelings now die
This outcome is now clear, I will not cry.

Run and Hide

Your muscles hurt, so tired, out of breath
Don't stop, their catching up, keep up the pace
Ignore away those pains, there's no time for death
No time, this is a never ending race
Don't go there, throw that in front of your path
Hide right behind that corner, have no fear
No time, you have to much worry of its wrath
Keep running and running from that single tear
You continue to run as it chases
You try and hide though it never stops seeking
But you're to slow, can't keep the paces
You look through your shaky fingers still peeking
This is something you will never escape
Your memories are here and it's too late

Journey Home

On off, on off, yellow, black, yellow, black
This is all you see staring at the light
Your life has changed with the sound of a smack
Amazing how lives change in just one night
You were going home drunk and ignorant
The rain was hard and your vision not good
He was going home just as innocent
Now the results lay splattered upon the hood
Time frozen, no longer coming to pass
Horrific scene burned into your mind
Time comes back hearing a knock on the glass
Paramedics are here scared what to find
One stays behind, one does not, this their fate
Now ones journey home is a journey never to make

Lost One

Become ash to ash, dust to dust
The end is near, this you must always fear
Our fate is sealed, this you know, this you must
Something you hold dear can never stay here.
They leave this world, go to another place
No stopping this day, no matter what you may
Memory gone only remains their face
Ultimate price to pay, nothing left to say
Now what? What can be done? What will you do?
New insanity gain, a whole new pain
Look upon their grave, nothing left for you
The heartache insane, standing in the rain
Let your heart heal and those memories fade
Live your life for them; you're the one that stayed

No Home.

Darkness of night, such a beautiful sight
Running through the darkened woods, all alone
So quite, so peaceful, everything seems right
No hostility, harm or thoughts of home
Look up, moon crawling across cold night sky
Time still continues, there is no escape
Your thoughts begin to race, try not to cry
Must return to that place, that place you hate
Thoughts of not going back, maybe even death
Entering your mind, growing like a seed
You come to a stop, now catching your breath
Thinking of others, those who are still in need
Mother, sister, brother they are the reasons you stay
Have no fear, no worry, soon will be your day.

Passion

The passion and lust I can not control
The feelings of want that will not subside
They spread through my body making me whole
Overflowing my mind, a rising tide

The touch of skin to skin a sensation
The spark traveling through your body a must
Minds becomes body from the exploration
No concern of trust, complete and utter lust

The souls unite slowly becoming one
The bodies move to the rhythm of night
Worries of mind becoming undone
Everything just perfect, everything right

Each others thoughts now burst forth, pure pleasure
You collapse, this moment you'll always treasure.

Tear

So very sad, tear running down your cheek
Worry of things starting to get to you
Everything has been building up all week
Sadness the only thing you know as true

It spreads through your body making it heavy
It spreads through your heart making it crack
Always of guard never being ready
Always hitting you hard with one big smack

Have no worries, have no doubt, have no fear
Let go upon this cold lonely night
Let the feeling flow, wipe away the tear
Those not willing to feel, a sorrowful sight

Tear your heart open to pain and sorrow
Have no fear, your heart will heal tomorrow.

Rain and Shine

See them walking hand and hand down the hall
Feel the anger start welling up inside
Realize your defenses are about to fall
Look the other way in hopes you can hide
Thinking of the times you had together
Remembering the feelings to still hold
Wondering why you thought it meant forever
Forcing your heart to grow so very cold
You had to let her go it was only right
Two different people not meant for each other
Let her drift away; no need for a fight
No matter what don't say you still love her
As long as she's happy deal with the pain
Let her day shine even if yours must rain

Larissa Williams

Who Will Hope in the One?

I.
Who will hope in the one
That seems to be perfect but goes to his castle
And creates flashbacks of painful memories
Of his way of expressing how much he loves his wife
Who will hope in the one
That allows herself to stay in the situation
The one that was a victim of abuse for years
And doesn't know how she will survive on her own
Who will hope in the one that doesn't realize every tear
their child has shed
Because of the arguing...
Who will hope?

II.
Who will hope in the one
That gets his high on the suffering and screaming of others
Who will hope in the one
That takes something so precious in minutes
Without the consent of the victim
The one that never fit in
And seeks his revenge on those weaker than him.
Who will hope in the one
That does a crime that deserves life but
Only receive 5 years.
Who will hope in the one
That was hurt his entire life and the only way
to get rid of the pain is to hurt others
who will hope?

III.
Who will hope in the one
That is a present day junkie but in the past a scholar.
Who will hope in the one that uses the piece of papers that comes
on the first to support her habit rather than support her kids
Who will hope in the one that looks like a cheetah
And fast like one when she doesn't have enough money to get a fix
So she goes and steals but gets caught. Who will hope in the one
that is completely different from what was expected. In the
morning she was getting A's and B's
But now all she's getting are those Z's. Who will hope in the one
That couldn't stay clean so that her unborn child wouldn't be an
addict
Who will hope?

IV.
Who will hope in the one that never had a chance
assumed at first glance
was only expected to know the meaning of gangster
and knew that he had a better be one
The one that thought it only mattered of how powerful his fists
were rather than his words.
Who will hope for the one that tried so hard to stay away but
Realizes that the death of others meant the life of him
Who will hope in the one
That had no father or mother
Not because of their physical absence
But the presence of drugs
Who will hope in the one that knew it was better to be apart than
against
Who will hope?

V.
Who will hope in the one
That has been beat in one family to the next;
The one that tries so hard to stay in the shadows
But always ends up in the light?
Who will hope for the one that can't be with his family;
But instead lives with someone that knows his worth and not his
name;
The amount they get for keeping him there
Who will hope in the one that never knew what it felt like to be
loved?
Who will hope?
Who will hope in those that can't hope for themselves
Those that don't want any hope from others
Who will hope in the one that has no more hope

The question isn't who will hope,
but who will help?

L E

At
one
point
in this
massive
whirlwind
of time, I
had a gold
fish. He
was
white
and probably
a she but he
still played
the role
of a
goldfish
pretty
well
even in death.

Jumping Trees: The Proximal Pursuit of Happiness
[Excerpt 1207]

The events disclosed are of natural existence and I will fight for the right to share them for they are what gave this journal life; yes for those asking, I am thanking the self-indulgent pricks who shipped me and others like mine self off to the island, without them there would be no need for my ostentatious battle of words here on paper.

It was a cool summer night in the middle of the month of June about a week after my seventeenth birthday. Our attempts of separation were proven to be as weak and frugal as the two of us may have been secretly hoping; we were indeed trapped in our little bubble of secrecy; far too indulged in the stinging solution to want out even though bursting the bubble then would have saved us both a lot of energy down the road when everything reached a new level of hardness. With our bodies bathed in half lit shadows, we cast very hungry looks and penetrating stares. Her words pierced me that night, deep and ardent; possibly the soul reason as to why I remember them like I remember the sun; like I remember her knock at my door, *click, click, clank*; like I remember the sound of her footsteps, all thirty of them from the master's quarters to mine, their rhythmic swish-swash against the marble floor; like I remember her hand in mine as I pulled her through the door; like I remember my heart's beat, its arrhythmic malfunction as she said her words into the very center of my ear quieter than I'd ever heard the wind.

And she said:

The Girl: Do mine eyes defeat me on so hollow
      A night to find thee coupled loosely with
      Mine own self singly in cold air? Speak you.
      Shed light as thou sees fit, for mine self finds
      It impossible to continue 'ere.

Me: It is right my lady. Thou have landed
      Here in quarters be known as mine. What say
      You with this? Arte thou no longer willing?

The Girl: Willing? Willingness ne'er leaves me. For I
      Am that but that which is not incomplete.
      See you that light? Lift it from its hold and
      Take out that shine it so brings forth. For now We must

be in nothing but our darkest
Shadows. Come o'er here with the scent of you
Touching me first; be my love without wed.

Me: Ay, yes me lady. Tonight I marry
The thought of you. Break me not, or so 'tis
Done.

The Girl: But done is nothing that does not start.

Me: Procrastination will not move me. Please,
If there is but one let it be you. Start
Or not, twill in me still be so. Relax
Let hear not you breathe if breathing is out
Of fear my love. These breaths are delicate
And we are all those gods' little creatures;
Created together. Come now. Let us
Be one again. Fear not tomorrow
For it is just tonight's distant fiend.

And this is not where it begins; the battle of the mind's conflictions of what is, for us and them, to have completely without fear of dominance showing *his* god forsaken little face and shoving his little fists over all but himself because in his self, Sir Dominance sees the almighty rule-writer and moral creator; and he completes his job as unjustly as he can get away with, (seeing that his little viral tube of airborne brainwashing failed when it touched those with immunities; those freethinkers who will not back down; those who aren't scared). It is known, and no one can say it is not, they hate us and our actions; but they sure as Hell's unlit fire will get off and on to get a few moments inside of our purity. To commence in their actions would only prove the nation correct in what they will not admit; witches in their naked truth reveal more than a few threats of containment and eternal mediocrity will force them to subscribe with their own blood upon their predators pearly white-stained parchment.

And in this moment I remember her thoughts becoming mine.

Is it my reluctance that has stranded
Me here bound by shackle and mine own self-
Righteousness; my inability to
Commit mine self to what I have heard from

Minds much more greater than mine own, to be
The inappropriateness of those un-
Kempt Saints who have been banished to the small
Island of the mistaken appalling
People; those whom did not fit the bill of
What is acceptable and what is not?
Am I to contradict myself now and
Go against my willingness to let her
Love me fully without fear? I am scared
Of what may come of this.

Hearing them, her thoughts, I almost shattered. She was unsure which was acceptable for her to be for she was the wife of the master and I was just the rebellious female slave, but I could not let her fear herself any longer. I took her close in my arms, introduced her to the physique of my shadows, placed my lips across hers, tongue twisting with hers, and in that moment she looked up into my eyes, defeated the inches of height distance, age distance, role difference, she became my equal; our completeness was sound.

Me: Please don't be scared.

coliz[un]

Let's take a trip

back to the place where
cherry boulevard splits

and

sit down in our 'ittle reefah
seats, light a few and get
bent up |all transfixed, displaced|
from this place [mosey] to the

next

.laugh at me for saying 'mosey'.
I'll still let you go back with me
to that day when we sat on the
sidelines, because our legs were
too short and our brains to slow
to dodge the five red balls

coming

at us like Ritalin and x, where
we sat waiting for the next
catch. pass|drop|hit to put us back
on the floor for round two or four
to score a few mates as we laughed
in the other teams face 'cause our
shortcomings were better.. or
at least we knew how to fix

them

each time we were allowed to step
on the wooden floor because that
was where the inner stuff that kept
us thriving was derived and the
con.sequences of ir.actions were
all conclusive 'ittle dabbles [dips]

diivess into nothing but retracted
innocence slipping and sliding across
our skin because no one actually knew
the diversion we were living or

where

to begin in trying to even name it
'twas a sin to be 'gainst what they
saw and did.. but time was traveling
freezing in their faces and the baby
who knew, was just pissing all around
causing a scene to be seen or maybe
she just had to pee and didn't know
how to not do it yet : whatever the matter,
the effect was still caused by the
unaffected |afterthought| 'I heart you'
and 'here is my card' dinner? yeah,
that prolly would have gotten a better

response

or some sort of revival.

peel

she runs up to her little screen
rubber stripping rubbing naked
leaving smears
a cheek a tear
fogging up the view
half scene

> come back to me
> come back to me I hate your guts
> I hate your guts on top of me
> let me breathe
> let me breathe into your face
> swallow me in filth
> I don't need you – I'm a caged monster
> let me devour you
> spread out wide spread
> images of the demon spawn
> giving birth to me
> pumping down the hallway on the little bicycle
> going nowhere except the nowhere coming close
> and the [and the] sounds I'm hearing
> just leave me alone
> I wanna live . I wanna leave .
> but still I want you to spread me on your sandwich
> bite me chew me . oh please don't throw me up
> I can't go back –the acid is my friend
> I'm bent like hell . just [just] give me a little bit
> and I'll leave you alone

half seen blocking my view
she wants the one right next to her
look at all she'd do
free her
she's sliding . back against the mirror
reflecting out the window
face carved perfectly
and still she's carving
licking and rubbing
rubber down her throat.

USofL: Re.Wolf

ha
aye look
a.not.her
lite.tell
flower
    bendoverpickup
    bringclosetoface
smelliTtit

8|p.p.p.p.p.p.p.p.p.p.p.p.p..pete.pete.peterrrr.retep}

onli
c of peter
would distress
the repressed
thought[s]
longer
than we ever
really wanted
to deal with
if wanting
was ever a
part
of us [to.be]
sparingly sharing
the key to the
inner
we.blazin
roots
to bite more
win more
see more
keep more
complete

8|p.p.p.p.p.p.p.p.p.p.p.p.p..pete.pete.peterrrr.retep}

iTs yellow
and iTs empty
weigh.ton.less
use.less
even
before

i picked iT up
just to
smell iT
i knew
it all along
yet i still
plucked
it from
its home

i knew it too
but i wasnt gonna
stop the giant hand
coming down for
me

i have no voice
i am but
a
re.wolf
everyone
else calls a
flower

three 15

somewhere   on   the   planet   earth

where the Son [shining b.right.] meets the water three times a day and wears the hell out of his orange liver [ticking tickly] tick brace.let just to let in a fresh breathe.E-Zzz.breeze underneath the vulgarity of sobriety sucking sweetly on his pulssSEeaaAwkwardly plea[s]ing / [the] optimissim erecting from his retractions and orderly factions of the sanity dis.placed [interjected.injected.injested.dejected.digested] between the blue and purple pea.pee.pill boxes / freely Swangin' [sangin'] like the cow who jumped over the one yellow Moon that grazed the hills of [an] Alternate Past across the street from an Interspecies bar [Galatea ukniight] the best nymph sea nerd so far...

at   threeFiFthTeen   threefifthteen   three.15

...a nonmilking baby cried out and matched his pitch thus far like the so far... complete / and i was GoiNGgoiNGgoooooN.e for the long haul around the bend of my dir.tea.est [allusionary] sins /peck.ing peace[fully] persistent at the eyes of a soaring sore.ring soooooooooooooooo.ring eagle in the sky who was up so dammmmmn HiGH that i could feel theweightlift off my.shoulders, fall quickly down and crumble into the mouth of the BuSHhh / remnants of the shhsh... shocking|my|seashells that i got from the she|at|the|shore. / who was just lookin' iNtoo...

the eyes of the seaman |shuttering| foulsfallfalsely [the phallicphalliciesfreefallin'] formably fighting false satisfaction around the pat.tell.ah that holds him together... he's breaking at his knees

A.L.t.M

..iM more than the
extra.tear.rest.trial
melting.pot -
smelling like old
sea.men -
propped up
against this rugged
doorway
waiting for you to
unwrap the goodies
at my feet

my fingers just
press the butt.ons
it's the fast air
that makes the music
a worthy musical
with its
musical
wrongness
which makes
it
right because
upside
down bananas
would
be the right side
up
of wrong
if my iEyes didnt
force everything to be seen
180 degrees
from its true
position
that's onli
true
if one believes
in equality
and not dictated
decrees
which decrease
the free motion
of particles
and kinetic energy

and that's like anti-physics
restraining the physique

iM more like
a
technicality
of
emotional abnormality
cause
i got aaa head full
of nonsense
two decades
minus three years of
brainwashing
and a
fish who likes
to play with sharks
in salty water
at high tide

iEye ride bulls
as my main source of
transportation
with the ticketing ticketors
tracing my trail
to see a trick
unfold bbetweeenn my lips
fingertips
stroking the cash nestled
between the clip
as i let it slip
to my lighter
as thc laughter
of another
round of the no touchin
game rings in my
ears

what a wonderful day
mum
yeahh
what a wonder.full day
is what i would say
if i could say
what ive wanted to say
since the first lay..

6R

Please, please, please....no

A wave of horror rushed through
His eyes..
Rage[d|d]Anger
Mist in the awakening
Shadowing the Mass.K.cuLiNE
Features of his flesh
Devoured power – his power
Burning through
Her imposed respect
The catalyst

She shook her head....no

RevitalizeRetributionRespectively
Did you...did you do it
Like you said you would
We should – I could..?

Body heating up
Stripped of innocence
Moving closer
Forcing [force]
Pushing [scar.red]
Him back [in.SiDe]
More and more
Into the dark depths
Of the forest walls
tHoSE(that WMD)WooDs
Lost in [theforebodingfollicles] TrEEs
Light, moonlight, sparingly sprouting
Puddles across her
Batteredbloody skin
He frightened.figureless,
Enveloped [more.so] by HiS
Own [dark]ness
Than that of natures
Neglectful caress,
Shuttering, loathing in Regret

She wasn't who she was
Or ever wanted to be
bButt.oOnn.tThiss.nNightt

She stood 67 inches high
Towering over the frame
Of the biggest
Dick
She had ever known,
Glorified in the Ressurected
Demeanor of her inner heroine
But still transfixed
In this world she grew up in
Quite alone besides
The company of him;
Her mentor, shelter, father;
Her life,
Appropriately Reassembled

Incapably.capable
In her inert approach
Ostensibly disconnected
She [made] him
Feeble.genuinely SoRreeY
But forgivness was no longer
An [theonly] option

He unknowingly.knowing
Transformed her
Into a homicidal.creature
The most insane of preachers
Into
HImself.myself.she.me.I
Had awakened

USofL: iSpilt MyShelf

iEye was a travel.linger
Traveller searching for the four
Sigh.iEye.did fur of for.got.ten
Faults flipping off two
Feign.girl.less hands

The Route was SixTeen,
And the blackc.l.ock read 0000 when
My two water.legs had put me
On that route to Sir.BiBiLL
A survival town of sorts
Where iEye'd bee zee
Ring lead.her of the
Hibiscus Flower
Pouring my Lost pride
For keeping the key in the
Fame.ill.E
Because my initials are L E
And Malaysia
Ain't got nothin' on me
But the South China Sea,
umm cause
iM not divided into two parts
iTs more like three..
Two, the power of me

turn it down turn it down turn it down
the music
the music

r u n n i n g

up my arm
all fast passed but
spaced out
the words in the soup
kitchen full
of old meat
old beat meat
old meat beat
to a pulp
the pulp in my juice
pulping pumping
pulsing through

my blood
the indigo indian
flavored lust
latching onto my tongue
as i

Y..A..W..N

R.U.B

SNiFF

Scratch
the scab pulling off beneath
my fingers
Damn my luck
it's bleeding

The TunnelSign said USofL
Twentea9iNe feet
But the Wagon in front of me said
The best of theUSofL right here
ZeRoW feet
My feet inched right along side as
My iEyes stretched to get
a look inside

Git..'er..done

What the hell..?

Ka blamm E

A Welcome Wagon
Tagged USofL
exploded right beside me
and my hands were
still attached to the
chemicals that made it happen

Ah the innocence shattered as
iEye was just walking through
the door....
Where the sum of all the numbers is
Seventy four
Minus 4OUR

Halo as in Halo

I feel like
sticking tampons [iNmy]
iEyes to have aa close.r
view of them swelling
protruding

in.flicting the
aureoles
with the choice
to choose or
not to choose
to stand erect
and watch this
display

this
heroism
pan out and
over

_____

under

the [un]outted
colossal
of what is
better identified
as dignity

experience
this degradation
of self
and self's
parts
cause self
doesn't see
self
slipping
out of the
zoooooooooone

the surreal|nor|the benign

into
just plain
asinine
see

self
asked
for
orange peels
and green leaves
on
self's
left toe

self said
"let there be"

and there was

self is indeed
deity to me

even if self's
halo
is yoked around self's
neck

self needs not to survive
to be alive

Author X

I'm just rousing.

It's all here on paper,
Hidden in metaphors and ambiguously
Indirect fragments, the story of me
But the unsightliness isn't diminishing
Or fading out of view
And I don't feel
Free
Instead,
Anxiety is breeding in my impediments
And the cloak of insecurity
Is tightening around my frame
And even when I draw it in closer
I can't shake this agitated state-
These vertiginous thoughts,
Spinning out of
Control-
From fear of you reading these words
And knowing
Me...
So I searched for a niche to crawl into
But nothing seemed to fit me
And my various accoutrements.
It was then I knew I had to choose-

In that moment, I let the cloak fall to the ground
And stood bare-skinned and leafless
Reveling in the repugnant pungency of who I am,
As is

White Li.n.es

She exists in the
interstitial space
amidst unfiltered emotions and native notions-
controlling actions and
pervading my reality,

and reverie.

When I'm tired of hiding behind a facade
and white lines are calling
I'm confronted with her image,
a reflection-
She views the world with scrutiny and asperity
suppressing the transient parcels of the past,
almost carefree...
Meanwhile I'm hoping to make these effects last,
seeking refuge from randomness,
but reluctantly descending
into the impending depths of
relentless infernal regions,
ancient history confronted once again.
if I could just inhabit *her* for a moment...

Then suddenly
she emerges and merges
into me
a rush of confidence
reverberating
and
radiating...

With powder on her nose.

Tuning In

Seeking translations otherwise impalpable
The surrogate satellite's stationary spins

Cautiously clashing in colors
SplashingMergingMeldingFusing
To the collective
we.her.me.I
Autopilot engaged
propelling.me.straight.forward
With the flip of a switch...

The empty orbs are gone
Instead, illuminated by articulate tongues, selves reincarnated,
Dedicated to deciphering the disciple, dead after only a decade-
Transposing thoughts, expounding meaning, illustrating
impurities
Otherwise concealed and suppressed- rendered useless.
But today, they mutate clearly through the cohorts who never
shut up-

I, the minion's host
Interpret the world-
My world
Our world-
Through metaphors, riddles spinning round the satellites-
(Seeking
Answers.Control.Identity.Validation...)
Come up static and empty-handed every.time

But never
Alone.

Invisible

I close my eyes to the world,
maybe if I don't see
them
they wont see
me

a naive
foolish notion
that I secretly wish worked...

like the sunglasses that make me invisible-

Reverse Peristalsis

She was always
Seeking the paragon
Of purity in perfection
Knowing it was preposterous.
But in her distorted mind
Intellect was
Waisting aweigh...
Nothing was ever gained
Except deception
In the form of a gold coin
Worn round her neck
Signifying the accomplishment
Of keeping it down.

And with that, they labeled her
Cured.

Stifling Femininity

Scantily clad, they are
Temptresses parading by-
Insinuating sexuality gives them power...
Flaunting, begging,
Lusting for love and affection,
Instead of thinking for themselves.
Negating their predecessors, slowly
Grating the framework for

Femininity that took years to build-
Enticed instead by masculine acceptance...
Masturbation's value is once again underrated
Indecent liberties occurring all around us
No longer limited to nocturnal emissions...
It's taking over, this
Nightmare of 24/7 prostitution, the
Innate defects of character of those who insist on
Tempting society to only see curves,
Yielding to the domination we've fought to overcome...

Impure Acts of Retribution

Infected with your games of
Manipulation and seduction
Professing pleasure when it's really power- I am
Unclean and seeking redemption,
Reparations for the acts that left me
Empty and licentious, with an

Anger that breeds self destruction...
Chastised by those who don't understand the
Terror instilled in victims of
Sexual abuse.

Overwhelmed with guilt
Feeding into shame and

Responsibility for actions no one could control
Even perpetrating the same learned
Tragic deeds on others
Repeating the cycle, reparations for
Impeded healing, and
Being forced to deny the
Undeniable- left
Trembling with trepidation
In a once peaceful dream, fairytales shift-
Once upon a time becomes once again, and
Nothing ever changes that...

Traffic

The Instituted process creates an incomplete half
as we are Pawned for the purpose of procreation
donning libelous Labels, adhering to the norms, conventions
indelibly Engraved at birth, graciously
accepting the Delineated roles mapped out
assigninG gender roles to gen.I.talia, another
commodity to Effete, meanwhile wo.men strive
to
eliminate
the
social
system
that
creates
sexism
and
gender

A Symphony of Emotional Release

Numb
A vacant void unable to feel
And make this real...
A crescendo of frustration building
Then it happened-
Urged by instinct, a shard of glass is moving about my skin in
sonata-allegro
form.
Scarlet beads rising to the surface,
Dis...con...nec..ted
But ever increasing in size
Until the billowing pearls became a constant trickle...
A rapturous release
And I was hooked,
An aficionado
Anxiously anticipating the orgasmic exsanguinations
Of the next movement...

It became an affair of sorts...
An adagio-
Graceful, well-controlled...
Finding the right instrument,
The right space with which to conduct the melody
That will execute this absolution of sin
Bringing deliverance from this evil
Festering within me

And finally I FELT
        pain
free
To compose a scherzo of lacerations waltzing across my skin
This way and that
Without hesitation
Until a rondo of indelible scars
Is all that was left
Distilling me
Bringing purity.

Hiding

Mama told me
I'd be a pearl
soon enough,
but she also told me
Jesus was
the way to go

I've stayed
coiled in my shell...
been washed up
on shore
to bask in the sunlight
content
sloshing about
drifting...

until I became
the ultimate shell
of a woman
submitting to the
accepted paradigm-
The kind of woman who
orders everything
by catalogue
the kind of woman
people haven't seen face to face
in years

all they ever get is
my small
pale hand
drawing back the curtains-
middle finger to the world
in my little
washed up dreams

September's Son

Seeping into me every year
as the September sun fades

seductively subtle
sauntering around me,
like a shop girl,
persisting, insisting
but I'm resisting her pleas
to change

I become me
the
wilted withering wallflower
that doesn't quite blend...
amongst the Lilies,
a real tumbleweed
pulled from my roots
by the harsh audacity of
f..........
a........
l.......
l......
.....
driven- rolled about
by the w i n d
aimlessly wandering, wondering
while that pop.you.liar
stream of consciousness
drifts past every October
...November |halts|
[thank you December]
with the refracted reflections
in store windows
toting the invitations
of preciousness and
precocious precariousness,
that wears like vintage fashion
on the minds of the hopelessly ordinary
who've never
felt
anything beneath the surface.
I don't need your under.standing
or pieces of your kindness,
sacked, like brittle glass beads.

I've got my protean-self to
reinvent;
like last decade's jeans.

Mrs. Easter's Students:

Lashami Morrison

Malika Davis

Terrell Corprew

Keimara Greene

 Marquese Hall

Michael penny

Kyshma Umstead

Tre Padgett

Steven cockerham

Melody Fuller

Kristina Allen

Tyler Burgette

Akilah Govan

Terrance Lyons

Abimael rubio

Kristen Schmidt

Alecia Cureton

Monet Wise

Shamia Allen

Jenne Gonzales

Tamika Robinson

Nnamdi Ukpabi

Devonte Johnson

Asia Jackson

"The Beach"
By Lashami Morrison

I wonder how it's going to be.
As I put down the window I hear
The wind whispering in my ear.

As we get on the beach,
My feet are on fire as I
Walk on the sand.

I see the ocean eating the fish
While waves come upon the shore.

As I pick up shells from the beach
The sun smiles down on me.

As time goes by, we leave and
Head back home.
As I look outside,
The city lights make me go to sleep.

"I Am From"
By Malika Davis

I am from a place where people walk all night
Trying to find some crack they know they shouldn't use

I am from a home where stuff is not always good—
Fussing and fighting all night long...

I am from a family that plays and jokes all the time;
Like my momma always says, "You think you a dime"...

I am from a neighborhood with many gang members
And a noisy lady named Mrs. Lucile that keeps her ground...

I am from a place where I keep childhood memories hidden
Because you have a lot of noisy people that are too sneaky...

I am from a house where people leave dog bones, cigarettes,
and everything in your yard.
There is just no respect.

I am from all of these moments, and I cherish them.

"Driving"
By Terrell Corprew

The car was black
It was like a trickster on wheels—
Fast to the crowd but
Really it was the smile of the bumper
That set it off, some thought.
It was the style of paint or the wheels that rocked.

"In Times Like These"
By Keimara Greene

I'm looking for a shining star that will show me the way to life.
I am so hurt from all of this pain.

I'm getting tired of everyone trying to put me down.

I'm letting too many people get close to me.

I am watching for danger in my life that is creeping in
Like a kid trying to steal a cookie.

I try to let my pain and stress go out the window.
I'm waiting for something good to come my way.

I am pressing a hot iron into my life to make it hard
And strong like a rock.

I'm trying to move on and stop
Letting little things hold me back.

I'm almost there—
Still looking for that shining star.

"Listen to Me"
By Marquese Hall

Listen to me,
Why don't you?
Yeah, you can hear me,
But you're not listening to me.

You don't trust me—
I can tell by the way you look
Every time I speak.
You judge my words.
I want to scream.
I want to cry.

My emotions are all bottled up.
If I let them out you'll be asking me questions
I won't want to answer.

Leave it alone.
It would all be over if you just
Listened to me
Sometimes.

"Boring"
By Michael Penny

School is boring everyday
But it seems like it gets even
Longer every week.

You do your work without speaking aloud.

You follow the rules without messing up.

You try to pass the class even though you don't care about it at all.

"Bad Weather"
By Kyshma Umstead

My window cried as the rain hit it.
The rain yelled, "Help me, help me!" as it hit the ground.

The clouds were screaming in horror as the lightning came.
The house's ears began to hurt as they heard the thunder.

"Death and Birth"
By Tre Padgett

Glass balls and glowing lights are hung
On a dead tree in the living room
We kill a tree to honor a birth?

"Stand Up"
By Tre Padgett

Stand up on your feet
Let people know you're here
Have a sense of pride
And let go of this fear
Use the mind God gave you
Do what you know is right
Follow the footsteps of your dream
And take part in this fight
You have a choice in life
You can ride or you can drive
I love you
But it's your choice

"Pass the Note Down"
By Steven Cockerham

I use common sense to decode lies
Surely you can't depend on rumors
When your smile suggests otherwise
Never leading on with the slightest frown
But surely your actions will bring you down
Revealing that you aren't truly what you claim to be
And soon enough people will se
They wonder if the rumors are true
And can they place the blame on you?
For broken relationships and affairs that transfix
Soon you're addicted, looking for your next fix
Commonly referred to as "easy"
But only by the dudes you play like a violin
Knowing lust is a sin
But you just can't keep your hands to yourself
Inhibitions put on the back of the shelf
Ignored while you indulge in *your own brand of friction*
"Fact or Fiction?"
Is no longer the issue
People realize the problem is you
And now they know these "so called" rumors are true.

"Pressure"
By Steven Cockerham

It wasn't long ago
When she had her own opinion
She used to be strong enough
To make her own decisions

But the adversity of high school
Has changed her perceptions
Negative views change the way
She sees her own reflection

So she tries her best to change
Rearrange what people see in her
She tries her best to reject
And deny the natural flaws in her

School books replaced by beer cans
Taken in to avoid rejection
Her life put at risk
For the sake of staged affection

Bottles of pills
Make her too lost to function
She's physically ill
On the path to self-destruction

People mourn her true self
Yet still hold firm to crazy measures
Why don't they face reality
And see if they could stand the pressure?

"What Am I?"
By Melody Fuller

I have no life—I just sit here all alone
With no one there
Someone may come around
And put their bottom on me
I carry more than 90% of bacteria
No matter where you go, I'm there—
The malls, your home, all the schools;
Trust me, I'm public
And you see me every day

"Success is the Journey"
By Kristina Allen

Success is the journey
Let's finish in four
You can accomplish your goal
Or even more

Make good grades
Like A's and B's
You can go to college
And earn some degrees

When you grow up
You could be a lawyer
Or be on TV
Just like Diane Sawyer

Success is the journey
Let's finish in four
You can accomplish your goal
Or even more

"Is Just"
By Tyler Burgette

A kiss is just a kiss
Till you find the one you love
A hug is just a hug
Till it's from the one you're thinking of

A dream is just a dream
Till you make it come true
And love is just a word
Till it's proven to you

"If You Could Walk in My Shoes"
By Akilah Govan

If you could walk in my shoes
You would see my life is not as easy as it looks

You see, I wasn't born with a silver spoon in my mouth
I wasn't born into the best family
If you were to walk in my shoes
You would see that they're not the best shoes
They're not easy to walk in
My shoes aren't fake—the pain is really there
My shoes are hard and beat up
My shoes aren't the best, but they're my shoes.

"Possibilities"
Terrance Lyons

I have good, bad, and crazy to the ground times.
I wonder sometimes about my African American men-
Why the heck we go against each other.

We were once slaves brought to America to work the farms...
Why must we hate each other? Is it because his cotton is better than yours,
Or is it because of crazy stuff like gangs, money, and power that niggas have?
When our pockets run dry will we blame it on each other?
Brother please, you're the one who put yourself in the spotlight and embarrassed yourself
I bet when a broken sista puts a freakin' dollar in your pockets to save your life,
You get weed, and think it's gonna suffice.
Nigga get up and find life and love.
If nigga's drop out of school- please, grab him and help him out.
If a nigga joins a gang
Please take him out and give him God.
If a nigga so much as touch a woman any kind of bad way
Teach him to treat her right.

Is it possible to change
Is it possible for man to fly
Or is it only possible for man to die?
I believe love will come across.
One things for sure,
We can love again through my possibilities.

"One Life is Too Short for Me"
By Abimael Rubio

How lovely it is to see you again
So goofy with the same look in your eyes

Like treasure kept beneath the earth
While above so simple, so plain
Destiny made sure I found that X on you
(It didn't give me a shovel though.)

Those days under the moon when we lay

Over the street
My question was the quiet night
Your answer was the shooting star

Getting lost on purpose was always fun
Until we couldn't find our way back home

Insults with smiles, playing cat and mouse
Was our thing because destiny made sure I found that X on you

"Where I'm From"
By Kristen Schmidt

I am from the busy streets
That always put me to sleep
I am from the old row homes
With nothing but a cement slab to play on
From the sound of ice cream trucks
That always came after dinner
From the old playground
That I never could use after dark

I am from the sound of my parents saying,
"You will become better if you try," and, "Never give up on what
you believe in."

I am from the old basketball cards
And sports on T.V.

I am another generation
And I intend to pass it on.

"Ballad of the Jacket"
By Alecia Cureton

Went to the store
Bought myself a jacket
It was too small
So I said, "Put it back, kid."

Tried on another one
It was too big
So I said, "Come on, man,
Just forget it."

Went to another store
They had the right size
It was kinda wet
But I wanted it dry.

Found another one
Nothing was wrong
So I bought the jacket
And I went back home.

"Cell Phone"
By Monet Wise

My cell phone asked me why I talk so much.
I told him it was just a habit.

I went to reach for my phone,
But he told me not to touch him until I pay my bill.

I told him he was the love of my life
And he replied that he was just a phone call away.

"School Fight"
By Shamia Allen

In class working hard
When I heard a loud scream
I went to the door
This had to be a dream

I saw people swinging
And jabs to the face
The principal came...
I had to get out of that place

I started running to the class
Before I got caught
Everybody yelling and screaming
Asking who had fought

I began laughing
Saying, "These people are crazy!"
It was uncalled for...but,
That fight really amazed me.

"Life"
By Jenne Gonzales

Let me tell you
Death is everywhere
Sometimes you don't feel
Safe anywhere

You have friends that
Don't like to share
And you see they
Don't really care

But now I desire
To straighten my life
And promise myself
Not to lie

Before another day
I pray God will save
Me and protect me
And always keep me safe

"A Place to Call My Own"
By Tamika Robinson

We're all looking for
A peaceful and safe place...

But maybe there's
No such place

Still we keep going no matter what's
Waiting for us down the road.
We don't stop living.

We will find that place—
Just keep looking
And you'll find it,
Someday.

"Me"
By Nnamdi Ukpabi

My heart is cold like ice
Don't try to love me
If so...
It will catch you in its vice

My mind is wide and vast
Like a giant maze
Don't try to understand me
Your patience will not last

"The Sky"
By Devonte Johnson

I love the sky when it's telling stories
When the neighborhood is full of worries
I also love when it cries and weeps
All of it puts me to sleep

"Morning"
By Asia Jackson

Early in the morning
Soon before dawn breaks
I look out of my window
Just as the sun begins to rise

I look over at the trees and
Morning dew glistens on the leaves
Making tiny rainbows dance
A special dance just for me

Then as I stand there at my window
I am serenaded by a small family
Of birds nestled
High in the tree

I begin to sway back and forth
As I listen to my private concert
Direct by nature
Just for me

The End.
[Unless you count the pages after this.]

www.ingramcontent.com/pod-product-compliance
Lightning Source LLC
Chambersburg PA
CBHW031827090426
42741CB00005B/158